MESSAGE TO THE AMERICAN

Clarence B. Leatherbury

Copyright

ISBN: 978-0-578-55964-3

CONTENTS

CONTENTS i
1 – ON ARTICLE VI OF THE US CONSTITUTION 1
2 – ON AUTOMATION 3
3 – ON BARACK OBAMA 7
4 – ON BUDGET DEFICITS 9
5 – ON COMMUNISM 13
6 – ON THE CONSTITUTION 15
7 – ON CORPORATE WELFARE 19
8 – ON THE DEBT CEILING 23
9 – ON EQUAL PAY FOR EQUAL WORK 27
10 – ON FEDERALLY-BACKED LOANS 31
11 – ON FREE SPEECH 35
12 – ON THE FREEDOM OF ASSOCIATION 39
13 – ON THE GENDER PAY GAP 43
14 – ON GOVERNMENT SPENDING 45
15 – ON ILLEGAL IMMIGRATION 49
16 – ON THE INCOME TAX 53
17 – ON INFLATION 57
18 – ON IRAQ 61
19 – ON ISLAM 65
20 – ON LIBYA 69
21 – ON THE MAINSTREAM MEDIA 73

22 – ON THE MINIMUM WAGE 75
23 – ON POLITICAL PARTIES 79
24 – ON PRESIDENT TRUMP'S IMMIGRATION BAN ... 83
25 – ON PUBLIC UNIVERSITY ADMISSIONS 87
26 – ON REFUGEE RESETTLEMENT 91
27 – ON SAVING 95
28 – ON SLAVERY 99
29 – ON SOCIALISM 103
30 – ON STATE NULLIFICATION 107
31 – ON SUBSIDIES 111
32 – ON SYRIA 115
33 – ON TAXATION 119
34 – ON THOMAS JEFFERSON 123
35 – ON TORTURE 127
36 – ON THE TSA 131
37 – ON THE UNEMPLOYMENT RATE 133
38 – ON THE UNITED STATES OF AMERICA 137
39 – ON VICTIMLESS CRIMES 141
40 – ON WAR 145
41 – ON WELFARE 147
BOOKS MENTIONED IN THIS BOOK 151
ABOUT THE AUTHOR 155

1 – ON ARTICLE VI OF THE US CONSTITUTION

On Sept. 20, presidential candidate Ben Carson was asked, “Do you believe that Islam is consistent with the Constitution?”

“No, I do not,” Ben Carson answered. “I would not advocate that we put a Muslim in charge of this nation.”

After this statement by Ben Carson, there was a massive outcry from Muslims and leftists across the United States. Nihad Awad, executive director of the Council on American-Islamic Relations, demonstrated his intolerant views towards anyone who speaks out against Islam when he demanded that Ben Carson withdraw from the presidential race. Then on MSNBC, Muslim Congressman Andre Carson stated, “The founding fathers as imperfect as they were ... were at least visionary in establishing Article 6 of the Constitution which states very explicitly that there shall not be a religious test to hold public office.”

First, Presidential Candidate Ben Carson never said that the US government should bar a Muslim from running for president. Ben Carson simply stated that he would not be advocating for a Muslim president. Congressman Andre Carson twisted Ben Carson's words by claiming Ben Carson wanted to violate Article 6 of the Constitution.

Perhaps, Andre Carson and Nihad Awad need some lessons on constitutional interpretation. The Constitution was drafted to restrict the federal government. The founding fathers inserted Article 6 into the Constitution to prevent Congress from instituting a state religion, as England had. Under Article 6, the federal government is not allowed to administer a religious test for those who want to hold office, but the American voter certainly has the right to take into consideration a politician's religion when casting his or her ballot.

2 – ON AUTOMATION

In a recent interview, Bill Gates remarked that robots should be taxed to curtail the displacement of workers by automation. Similarly, in his farewell address, Barack Obama warned that automation might lead to a wave of middle-class jobs becoming obsolete. These Marxian fears about automation are commonly expressed among politicians and the public alike. For example, lately Labor Secretary Nominee Andrew Puzder was publicly pressured into withdrawing his name from consideration due partly from his pro-automation stance.

However, is automation something Americans should fear? Karl Marx once cited the displacement of the English handloom weavers by machines as one of history's most horrific tragedies. However, if you ever watched Milton Friedman's PBS television series, *Free to Choose*, and witnessed the physical strain workers must endure in operating handlooms, you may conclude that the development of automated weaving machines was not, as much a tragedy, as it was a blessing. In an episode, titled "The Tyranny of Control," Milton Friedman arrived at a village in India called Anicaputar.

At this village, he witnessed hundreds of handlooms being operated by the poorest of the poor. In Anicaputar men, women, and children were toiling their lives away because government officials had enacted policies to protect them from getting displaced by automatized machines. Friedman explained, "By subsidizing the cotton that the villagers spin and the cloth that they weave, they made it difficult for the modern industry to develop."

However, what if India's government had never intervened and instead allowed the market to operate freely by its own devices? What would have ensued? India's weaving industry would likely have mirrored that of Japan's highly mechanized weaving industry. Without the enactment of protectionist measures by the Indian government, modern factories housing state-of-the-art machines would have supplanted the wooden handlooms that were scattered throughout villages like Anicaputar.

So, what of the workers you might ask? Well, author Thomas E. Woods provided us some relevant insight on this question in his work, *The Church and the Market: A Catholic Defense of the Free Economy.* Woods wrote, "But such machinery...allows the same amount of output to be produced by fewer hands, thereby releasing into the economy a supply of labor that can now be applied to the production of goods that we could not have had before because the requisite labor had been tied up..." He went on, "The additional goods produced by the additional labor have the happy result of raising real wages since an increase in the supply of goods available will increase real wages by endowing all real incomes with greater purchasing power."

Karl Marx was wrong. Friedman and Woods were right. Technological progress in automation, along with capital investments in new machinery, will only increase the productive capacity and efficiency of an economy providing an increasing standard of living for everyone.

3 – ON BARACK OBAMA

When I heard President Barack Obama at a campaign rally criticizing Donald Trump for speaking fondly of Vladimir Putin, I immediately thought to myself that Obama might be having an identity disturbance. In psychology, they call this psychological projection. It is where a human denies an aspect of their negative behavioral traits while attributing those traits to someone else. For how could Obama stand before an audience and criticize Trump for his diplomatic remarks toward Russian President Vladimir Putin, while Obama himself continually sells King Salman of Saudi Arabia billions of dollars' worth of weapons?

On Sept. 13, Obama spoke to a crowd in Philadelphia about Trump's comments toward Putin. Obama stated, "And now their nominee is out there praising a guy, saying, 'He's a strong leader because he invades smaller countries, jails his opponents, controls the press and drives his economy into a long recession.'"

When I heard the remark from Obama, it occurred to me that our president may have been subconsciously weighing his alliance with the Saudi Kingdom. Saudi Arabia is currently invading the smaller country of Yemen. And their government is notorious for arresting dissidents and rigorously censoring what information the media releases to the public. Obama disparaged Trump for offering kind words toward the Russian president, but I am afraid Trump's kind words cannot compare in consequence to the unkind bombs Obama offers the Saudi King.

4 – ON BUDGET DEFICITS

President Barack Obama has been stating in speeches that the annual budget deficit has gone down by three-quarters during his presidency. He can make this elusive claim by comparing the current budget deficit to the 1.4 trillion-dollar budget deficit run-up in 2009. Though Obama's claim is valid, I find it somewhat deceptive. For Obama to use 2009 as his reference point to gauge the present deficit levels is absurd. To demonstrate this absurdity, imagine a man lived a frugal lifestyle and spent $1,000 per year on his credit card for 20 years. Then in 2015, he lived beyond his means and spent $100,000 on his credit card. Then in 2016, he still lived beyond his means but only managed to spend $50,000 on his credit card. He then cheerfully boasts that his annual credit card deficit has gone down by half since 2015, all the while failing to mention how his 2016 spending levels still far exceed the yearly credit card liabilities he accrued customarily through years past or that his actual credit card bill is growing exponentially.

For example, Obama could mention how seven of the eight largest annual budget deficits in US history have occurred under his presidency. He could say how the $108 billion federal budget deficit for March 2016 is larger than the budget deficit for the entire year of 1996. He could mention how he has added more to the national debt than all previous US presidents combined. He could also mention how his administration has forecast the 2016 annual budget deficit to reach $616 billion. This $616 billion deficit will be around $157 billion higher than President George Bush's 2008 budget deficit, and it will be yet another 616 billion dollars tacked onto an already swelling national debt. And note, the $20 trillion national debt only accounts for bonded liabilities, but if one were to account for nonbonded (unfunded) liabilities as well the national debt would exceed 127 trillion, according to Vance Ginn of Forbes.com. In the book, *The Biggest Con,* author Irwin Schiff explained, "Unfunded government liabilities can be understood by considering the situation of a soldier discharged from service with a government pension... The government does not issue him a series of bonds which he must redeem each month." In other words, that pension is a liability that must be paid by the government. Yet that liability is not calculated into the national debt.

Politicians will contend that Americans should not worry because during years of prosperity, the national debt will be paid down, but this is fantasy. The Congressional Budget Office has already projected that by the year 2022, the annual budget deficit will surpass $1 trillion. In no small measure, this trillion-dollar forecast is due to

Washington's inability to reform entitlement programs such as Social Security, Medicaid, and Medicare. Just as significantly, it is due to Washington's endless appetite for engaging in military interventions overseas. Even during the budget surpluses of Bill Clinton's presidency, the national debt still increased annually because our elected officials did not have the discipline to direct those surpluses towards reducing the national debt.

5 – ON COMMUNISM

Bernie Sanders is not the answer. While he has been able to identify problems that face this country, he has been unable to offer Americans any real solutions. His solutions consist of more regulations, more taxation, more military interventions, more judicial activism, and more bureaucratic redistribution. However, if massively increasing the scope of government leads to prosperity, shouldn't the wealth of the American people be rapidly increasing after the drastic expansions of government under the Bush and Obama administrations?

While you are considering that question, I also want to bring up another qualm I have with Bernie. In *The Black Book of Communism*, published by Harvard University Press, author Stéphane Courtois estimates that communism caused 94 million deaths. Sanders has several questionable ties to this horrid ideology brought to light by author Paul Sperry in his New York Post column, *"Don't be fooled by Bernie Sanders — he's a diehard communist."* And since Donald Trump was called upon to disavow an organization he has zero ties with, I think it is only fair and proper that Sanders should be called upon to disavow communism.

6 – ON THE CONSTITUTION

Justice Antonin Scalia rightfully understood that when interpreting the Constitution, the Supreme Court had a duty to uphold the original intent of the document established during its ratification. Though today, strictly adhering to the Constitution is looked upon by large sections of society as primitive. So, in honor of the late Justice Scalia, I wanted to resolve the common misinterpretations of our Constitution, which have helped lead to the unfortunate state of our current republic.

First, it is Congress' constitutional responsibility to declare war. James Madison explained, "The Constitution supposes, what the History of all Governments demonstrates, that the Executive is the branch of power most interested in war, and most prone to it. It has accordingly, with studied care, vested the question of war to the Legislature."

Second, the tenth amendment assured that the powers states delegated to the federal government could not be expanded upon, except through the amendment process.

The states delegated specific enumerated powers to the federal government under Article 1 Section 8, but the lion share of powers was reserved to the states. However, one can easily see just how far the federal government has abused its powers when reading *Federalist #41* written by James Madison and comparing Madison's views about the role the federal government would play in society to present realities.

Third, the Supremacy Clause is not an unlimited grant of power. At the New York ratifying convention, Alexander Hamilton explained, "acts of the United States will be absolutely obligatory as to all the proper objects and powers of the general government... But the laws of Congress are restricted to a certain sphere, and when they depart from this sphere, they are no longer supreme or binding."

Fourth, the founders' understood that times change and as a result, they created the amendment process so the Constitution could be altered when needed. The Constitution was not to live and breathe through judicial activists. The Constitution was to only live and breathe through the amendment process.

Fifth, the first amendment limited Congresses lawmaking authorities but not the states. For example, many state constitutions endorsed Christianity, and the state governments provided financial assistance to their respective religious institutions. Note the words, "Congress shall make no law..."

Sixth, the general welfare clause did not expand the government's ability to spend money but constrained it. In the book, *33 Questions About American History You're Not Supposed to Ask,* historian Tom Woods described how "the word 'general' restricted federal spending only to those purposes whose benefits were national in scope rather than purely local or confined to a single interest group."

Thomas Jefferson understood that our liberties and wealth are more likely to be preserved by imposing strict limitations on the federal government. Jefferson duly stated, "On every question of construction, let us, carry ourselves back to the time when the Constitution was adopted, recollect the spirit manifested in the debates, and instead of trying what meaning may be squeezed out of the text, or invented against it, conform to the probable one in which it was passed."

7 – ON CORPORATE WELFARE

In 2013, Republicans in the Indiana General Assembly voted for an unsuccessful bill that would subject women receiving Temporary Assistance for Needy Families (TANF) benefits to drug tests. The Republicans garnished public support for this legislation by claiming it protected the taxpayer. However, all these so-called fiscal conservatives were engaged in nothing but some political trickery designed to make it seem as if they were looking out for you; when in reality they were causing economic harm to you.

The Legislative Service Agency put out a fiscal impact statement on HB 1483, which stated that the legislation would result in a net increase in state expenditures of $2.6 million its first year. The fiscal impact statement went on to say, "Actual revenue the state could receive from withheld TANF benefits for positive drug tests is estimated to be approximately $215,000." These Republicans who supported this bill told you and me it was going to save us money when the truth is this bill would have raised taxes by $2 million in its first year.

Before this law was declared unconstitutional in Florida, the Sunshine State drug-tested 4,086 TANF applicants, and only 108 individuals (2.6 percent) tested positive. So why did Indiana Republicans support this similar bill? The Indiana Republicans supported this bill because they knew it would rally segments of their constituency behind them. They supported this bill because it would lead to a pharmaceutical corporation being granted a lucrative government contract. They supported this bill because it means millions of your tax dollars would be given to the Indiana FSSA agency. They supported this bill because, in reality, they see anything that can swell the government's payroll as progress.

However, in this day of information, citizens are learning to see, think, and listen for themselves. And as those citizens become politically mature, they are no longer going to fall for any more of these political tricks. Voters will no longer give blind obedience to a party or a politician's propaganda. Their only obedience will be to the truth. And the truth is, it did not make any economic sense to support a bill that would have saved the taxpayer $215,000 from TANF beneficiaries failing drug tests when the bill itself cost the taxpayer $2.6 million a year to administer.

Republican State Representatives signed the Taxpayer Protection Pledge which stated they would, "oppose and vote against any and all efforts to increase taxes," but by voting for the costly legislation, your Republican representatives have broken their pledge to you! They have broken their oath to you!

Barry Goldwater once asked. "Where is the politician who has not promised his constituents a fight to the death for lower taxes—and who has not proceeded to vote for the very big spending projects that make tax cuts impossible?" In 2014, the Republicans General Assembly members were at it again working on passing another version of the bill known as HB 1351, but fortunately, that bill did not become law either. I hope these out-of-touch Republicans legislators can now see their hypocrisy. Moreover, I hope that in the future they will strive to kill any taxpayer eating, privacy-violating, and blood sampling Frankenstein their political cronies come up with next.

When similar legislation became law in Florida, Governor Rick Scott, who made his riches from the pharmaceutical and medical industries, wanted to give a state contract to a company, like Solantic, to test the 4,086 TANF applicants. I wonder what pharmaceutical company our Republican representatives had in mind to receive the state contract to test the Indiana TANF applicants. In the name of combatting social welfare, the Republicans are encouraging a form of corporate welfare.

Indiana government employee Greg McAloon (who is with the Family and Social Service Administration, which oversees TANF), makes a $7,344 a month salary, whereas, the maximum Indiana TANF benefit for a family of three is around $290 a month. Why should individuals benefit lavishly on bureaucratic welfare be exempt from the intrusive legislation when individuals on social welfare are not? Can you see the hypocrisy? Not that I am encouraging such a program since it would be yet another cost to the taxpayer.

I certainly understand the sentiment behind Americans wanting to drug test welfare recipients, but instead, these Americans should use their energies to advocate for the end of TANF altogether. Private charity from churches, family, friends, organizations, and charitable Americans can meet the needs of these Hoosiers that have fallen on hard times in place of the taxpayer.

8 – ON THE DEBT CEILING

Of late, the national debt has surpassed 18 trillion dollars. American independence is weakening as foreign ownership of US debt is mounting. If the national debt were to be paid off today, every American would owe over $56,000. Since 1962, the debt ceiling has been raised 74 times. Ronald Reagan did it eighteen times. George W. Bush did it seven times. President Obama has done it five times. So, history has blatantly proven that neither party has the competence to make the necessary cuts in government spending. I specifically mentioned competence because I have repeatedly heard our wise political overlords make remarks to the public regarding the debt that are a pure economic fallacy, which if not recognized, are capable of doing extreme harm to the American citizens' financial well-being.

For example, one of President Obama's favorite talking points is to suggest that a reluctance to raise the debt ceiling is equivalent to a customer who had ordered a meal and then decides to leave the restaurant without paying.

I find this analogy deceptive. A better analogy would be that Barack Obama, John McCain, and Nancy Pelosi force you to eat dinner with them at an expensive restaurant. Then once they get to the restaurant, they order up everything on the menu several times over, and then after the meal, President Obama reminds you that if you do not pay this bill they just racked up, the IRS is going to put you in prison. In this analogy, the expensive meal the politicians ordered without your consent represents the wars, illegal immigrants, foreign aid, welfare, government salaries, bureaucratic agencies, and subsidies that you are forced to pay for. Also, in my analogy, the expensive meal cost around twenty trillion dollars.

The only problem with my analogy is that you (the taxpayer) cannot afford the entire twenty trillion-dollar bill, so after emptying your pockets, Barack has to ask the nearest Chinese customer if he can borrow a few trillion. Though this is still not quite enough, so Barack tells Ben Bernanke, with the Federal Reserve, who just so happens to be sitting one table over, to print up a few more trillions to help finance the debt they racked up. Yet this still is not quite enough to pay for the meal, so Barack takes out another credit card from his pocket and asks the cashier to place the rest of the bill on it, along with a milkshake for the drive back home.

Remember, raising the debt ceiling means the government is just piling on more debt. Issuing larger debts to retire smaller debts cannot be described as paying off one's bills. The state could still meet its interest obligations by cutting waste from the budget, which would benefit the economy since scarce savings would be channeled back into the private sector, instead of being spent on government largess.

In their book, *Tyranny of the Status Quo*, Milton and Rose Friedman advocated a Line Item Veto and a Balanced Budget Amendment to help control spending. In it, they cited Thomas Jefferson for stating, "I place economy among the first and most important virtues, and public debt as the greatest of dangers to be feared...To Preserve our independence, we must not let our rulers load us with public debt." Jefferson remained true to his word by paying off the national debt during his presidency.

9 – ON EQUAL PAY FOR EQUAL WORK

Lately, when I listen to politicians, I will hear them advocate for Equal Pay for Equal Work legislation. The White House website claims, "full-time working women earn just 78 cents for every dollar a man earns." Of course, this is nonsense. If a potential male employee would require a $100,000 salary from an employer but a prospective female employee, of the same knowledge and skill set, can be hired for $78,000, who do you think would get the job? If there was a 22% premium to employ a man over a woman, doesn't it seem that the vast portion of our labor force would immediately start consisting of predominantly women? As to any discrepancy in earnings, economist Murray Rothbard stated in the *Individualist* that it was not, "sexist discrimination," which caused the discrepancies but rather that, "the overwhelming majority of women work a few years, and then take a large chunk of their productive years to raise children..."

In reality, the politicians that desire the enactment of Equal Pay for Equal Work legislation are being anti-women.

Hypothetically, imagine if a potential male employee applicant has more skill sets than his female employee applicant counterpart for a specific job opening. In such a scenario, the only way the female can compete for the position is by agreeing to work for less money. Without the law on the books, the woman might land the job by offering to work for a lesser salary. After receiving the position, she then could improve upon her skill sets and earn higher wages, due to her increasing productivity, over time. With the law on the books though, the employer would be forced to pay an equal salary for the available position, and as a result, will elect to go with the higher skilled male applicant. Due to the law, the female applicant will not be obtaining the valuable employment skills she otherwise could have received, which will only further widen the wage gap between her and the male applicant, who got the job.

The free market imposes a harsh cost on employers who engage in irrational discrimination. If in our hypothetical above, the woman is indeed more qualified but is not selected because of her sex, then that employer would suffer from not obtaining her superior services. Milton Friedman once remarked, "The free market, by enabling people to compete openly, is the most effective device that has ever been invented for making people pay for their prejudices."

Many other negative consequences stem from this type of legislation. Agencies which enforce such laws have proven to be very costly due to the monstrous tax and legal burdens they impose on society and business. The Equal Employment Opportunity Commission alone has a yearly budget of $355,000,000. The troves of dollars confiscated from the citizens by these agencies reduce the amount of private capital that could have been used for business expansions; expansions that could have led to more women hires. Also, taxes are a cost for businesses—a cost, which is then passed onto the consumer in the form of higher prices; higher prices, which in turn negatively impact the purchasing power of women.

10 – ON FEDERALLY-BACKED LOANS

President of Indiana University Michael McRobbie recently stated in his 2012 university address, "I want to make it clear that we have heard and shared the public's concerns over college affordability."

If McRobbie is genuinely concerned about college affordability, why has he continually accepted extravagant pay increases? According to the IU Salary Database, during the 2007-2008 school year, McRobbie made $400,000. For the 2008-2009 school year, McRobbie made $425,000. And now during the 2012-2013 school year, IU President McRobbie is getting a tax and tuition-based $544,848.00 a year salary. Comparatively, the President of the United States makes $400,000.

It is not just the University President that is being granted lavish tuition and tax-funded pay increases. Professors throughout the IU system are systematically receiving thousands of dollars in salary raises every year. In the IU Salary Database, I selected an accounting professor from the Kelley School of Business and analyzed his salary. In 2003-2004 the professor made $118,000. By the 2007-2008 school year, he made $142,000. And now during the 2012-2013 school year, he is making $177,000.

A lot of Hoosiers will make the argument that these big salaries are justified because we need "the best and brightest minds to come to our state and lead us." I do not buy their talking point. I know well-qualified lawyers and businessman from my community who would gladly take on the IU President's position for a respectable salary of $200,000 a year. The other bureaucratic argument is that the Indiana University's President's salary is in line with the wages that are paid out in other states. However, nearly every state in America ran a deficit in 2013. Indiana can be a leader in this nation, but to be able to lead, our state needs to be independent-minded. Indiana cannot afford to succumb to the failed budgetary policies of other states.

According to CollegeCalc.Org, in the year 2000, the undergraduate in-state tuition rate for IU Bloomington was $4212. By 2010, the tuition had doubled to $8613. Presently, the average loan debt for an IUB graduate is $27,752.

Author and renowned financial advisor Peter Schiff explained that Universities have been able to raise tuition substantially because of federally-backed student loans.

Because the government backs the student loans, there is not any financial risk for the private lenders in loaning out funds to risky applicants because the taxpayer will be on the hook for paying the loans back if the student defaults. In an article on SchiffRadio.Com, Peter Schiff wrote, "Easy access to cheap credit enables students to bid up tuition, benefiting the educational establishment at their expense. Politicians secure student's votes by promising relief from skyrocketing tuition by providing even more loans. Ironically, the loans themselves are the very reason tuition is so high in the first place. Before the Federal Government got involved, college degrees were much more affordable, and ambitious students from poorer families could easily work their way through."

11 – ON FREE SPEECH

Free speech is under attack. On April 28th, 2017, conservative Ann Coulter had to cancel her talk at the University of California, Berkeley, due to threats of violence. Her concern for her own and her supporters' safety was certainly justified after seeing what unfolded on February 1, 2017, when media personality Milo Yiannopoulos tried to hold a conservative talk at UC Berkeley. Milo was forced into an emergency evacuation after violent rioters swarmed his event. That mob hurled smoke bombs, beat Milo's supporters unconscious with metal poles, broke windows, set fires to private property, and threw Molotov cocktails at officers. These ever-more occurring acts of violence are prime examples of just how intolerant the radical left has become.

Presently, if an individual discusses problems that arise from an Islamic belief system, that individual is labeled Islamophobic. If an individual discusses issues that stem from mass migration, that individual is labeled xenophobic. If an individual is critical of the feminist movement, that individual is labeled a sexist. If an individual discusses problems within minority communities, that individual is labeled a racist. And, if an individual supports a noninterventionist foreign policy, that individual is labeled an isolationist.

These labels are un-American, narcissistic, mindless, and degrading. We have seen an uptick in the radical left employing such slander and physical attacks because they cannot win a policy debate based upon reason, evidence, and sound economic argument alone.

On April 20, 2017, Howard Dean tweeted, “Hate speech is not protected by the first amendment.” Dean’s tweet should be of grave concern to any free thinker, for there is no way to interpret what is classified as hate speech except by subjective means. Such laws would allow partisan officials to become the judges in determining what is classified as hate speech. It would allow the state to decide what its citizens can say versus what they cannot.

The radical left wants hate speech laws enacted to subject Americans to criminal penalties if they speak critically of certain groups. Hate speech laws are weapons used to suppress free speech, stymie debate, and bludgeon dissidents into submission. If you dare to think for yourself, you’re a threat to their rule.

Former Congressman Ron Paul often reminds Americans that the first amendment was not written to talk about the weather. Scientific inquiry, secularism, due process, and equality before the law were all once-fringe concepts, but open, rigorous debate turned such fringe concepts into today's western values.

If we want to pass the freedom of speech down to future generations and to continue advancing civilization, we must not become complacent in defending the first amendment against individuals and groups who are hell-bent on its destruction. On Freedomain Radio, Philosopher Stefan Molyneux teaches that free speech is the foundation of civilization. Molyneux remarked, "You see we have arguments or we have bricks, we have words or we have hammers, there is no third way."

12 – ON THE FREEDOM OF ASSOCIATION

This August, the Colorado Court of Appeals ruled that a bakery owner violated the law when he refused to bake a cake for a gay couple's wedding. And this past spring, an Oregon Judge fined a couple $135,000 for refusing to bake a cake for a gay wedding due to their Christian beliefs. When I read headlines like these, it makes me question the politicians who profess that we live in a free society. How can one proclaim to live in a free society if one cannot refuse to bake someone a cake without being subject to excessive fines and prosecution by the state? Unquestionably, the Revolutionary War was waged on the notion that our freedoms would extend farther than this minute realm.

Leftists routinely cite the separation of church and state when defending gay marriage against Christian objections to the state issuing marriage licenses to gay couples, but why weren't leftists citing this same doctrine to oppose state action against Christian bakers when refusing to bake cakes for gay couples? And leftists routinely cite the freedom of association in their support of the gay community to associate with whom they please. Yet when the principle of the freedom of association acts against the gay community, by allowing free individuals not to associate with gay marriage ceremonies, the same leftists are vehemently opposed. Such inconsistency makes me think their ideas are not based on principle as much as an agenda.

The First Amendment to the United States Constitution guarantees freedom of speech, but this freedom is gutted when the government cracks down on citizens for merely taking a stand not deemed politically correct. As author and CEO of Euro Pacific Capital Peter Schiff warned, “If the government can ban conduct that it deems offensive then it can also ban speech, writing, art and even thought for the same reason.”

Just as gays and lesbians desire to be able to practice a particular sexual orientation without being harassed, Christians do not want to be harassed, as well. In John 8:7, Jesus said, "Let him who is without sin among you be the first to throw a stone at her." To the purported progressives who routinely cast the word bigot at your fellow man, who desire to suppress the speech of which you do not approve, and who feel those who do not hold your views should be subject to financial ruin—you are the ones casting that stone.

If a couple is refused a wedding cake, their property rights are not being violated because they have no ownership interest in the bakery or baker's labor. There can be no voluntary exchange from the buyer and seller until both sides have mutually agreed to the market transaction.

It is not progressive that the state is now promoting involuntary servitude against Christians by threatening them with costly lawsuits if they do not obey their commands. Throughout history, Christians have been subjected to the most extreme atrocities, and by handing down such arduous penalties, history is repeating this unenlightened trend.

Progressives could learn from Malcolm X who explained, "If someone holds a gun on a white man and makes him embrace me—put his hand, arm, around me—this isn't love nor is it brotherhood. What they are doing is forcing the white man to be a hypocrite, to practice hypocrisy. But if that white man will put his arm around me willingly, voluntarily, of his own volition, then that's love, that's brotherhood, that's a solution." Malcolm's teaching is an example of freedom of association, in practice. Can't you see how the latter is ideal to the former?

13 – ON THE GENDER PAY GAP

The Current Population Survey conducted by the US Bureau of Labor Statistics found that women, on average, earn $36,278 annually compared to $47,127 for men. A 23% pay gap which the Obama administration habitually cites as evidence of discrimination by Americans. Though, if one was to analyze the numbers to discover the truth behind the disparity, one will find that there are several legitimate reasons why a gap exists that has nothing to do with sex discrimination.

First, according to the survey, women, on average, work fewer hours a week than men. Second, men work more overtime. Third, on average, women's job tenure is shorter than it is for men. Fourth, the CONSAD Research Corporation found that women value non-wage benefits more than men, and as a result, take a higher percentage of their compensation in the form of fringe benefits. A fifth reason there is a gap in pay is that men on average tend to go into careers that offer higher salaries, for example, engineering, mathematics, or computers, whereas women pursue lower-paying employment fields like healthcare or education. And sixth, a large portion of women must interrupt their careers to raise children.

These are the employment choices men and women make on their own accord. However, if leftist politicians and voters continue to disregard the truth, while habitually shouting the word “discrimination,” they will further damage the reputation of our honorable entrepreneurs and businesspersons who employ Americans, and they will swing election outcomes due to their misinformation campaigns to leftist politicians who have no business being in Washington.

14 – ON GOVERNMENT SPENDING

In America, there is a belief that government spending strengthens the economy. However, as a result of massive spending by the federal government; as a result of monetary policies leading to a dramatic devaluation of the dollar; and as a result of artificially low interest rates set by the Federal Reserve which encourage individuals to take on more debt, the average American now has a negative savings rate.

This lack of austerity by the US government has led to the offshoring of American manufacturing because these companies could not withstand the US storm of taxes and regulations while remaining competitive along with staying economically viable. The federal government's appetite for spending has also resulted in itself becoming highly dependent on foreign capital. The federal government now spends so many trillions it has to borrow from foreign governments to service its debt. This dependence on foreign capital will only further increase the taxation burdens here at home since these borrowed funds have to be paid back with interest. For example, in 2017, the federal government spent $263 billion on interest payments alone. And as a consequence of such dependence on foreign capital, America's national security has been compromised.

The Federal Reserve website says it implements monetary policy to maintain an inflation rate of 2 percent per year. Sadly, according to Free Market Economist Peter Schiff, the real rate of inflation is actually around 7 percent because the government downplays the actual figure. If you do not know whom to believe, look at the cost of groceries, healthcare, education, and war—then decide for yourself what to think.

Inflating the money supply hurts everyday Americans because it increases the cost of living and creates business cycles, but the government engages in this practice so it can pay back its many creditors without acting like its raising taxes on the public (though the public is paying the hidden inflationary tax). This fed tactic makes the national debt serviceable because it can be repaid with newly printed money versus being paid solely through real taxation.

The Federal Reserve also keeps interest rates artificially low, which benefits the federal government in managing its debts. Yet these artificially low-interest rates are a double-edged sword since such artificially low rates encourage increased borrowing from both the private and public sectors leading to more debt and malinvestments.

Two hundred sixty-three billion dollars of the American tax payer's money was spent on interest payments to service the national debt, but if only our government had balanced its budget every year, those billions could have been left in the private sector. As a result of federal borrowing from foreign governments, foreign governments today hold trillions of dollars' worth of US bonds. Eventually, those nations are going to cash them in and use the money to purchase American land, American businesses, and American politicians.

What can be done? The US government must make drastic cuts in spending across the board, and Americans must learn to save by engaging in less consumption. Since the citizenry would no longer be spending as much of their money on immediate consumption items, workers and resources would be diverted away from low paying service sector jobs (jobs that tailor to immediate consumption), towards industries engaging in higher-paying long-range production jobs.

The increasing pull of savings in the economy would signal to entrepreneurs to begin investment projects. The stemming investments would allow labor to be more productive, resulting in higher economic output in the market economy. As the capital is channeled back into the private sector of the economy and away from the public sector, the productive capacity of our nation would begin to grow. Soon America would once again be an economy that saved, produced, and created wealth.

15 – ON ILLEGAL IMMIGRATION

Why do you lock your door at night? Why do you not feed, clothe, educate, finance, and provide a bed for illegals who are of no family relation to you? We all know the answers to these questions. Why it would be absurd for you to dwindle your wealth on those illegals who do not love you at the expense of those who do. Why it would be foolish for you to leave your door unlocked putting your family's welfare in jeopardy.

And the same reason why you choose to lock your door is the same reason why the United States should lock its door to illegal immigration. When someone knocks on your door, you don't just open it and shout, "Come on in." You check to see who's there first. You want to make sure they're alright before you open your door and you're not wrong for doing this. You're not racist for doing this. You're smart for doing this. You're a man for doing this. And just as you have an obligation to stop visitors from overstaying in your home due to the extreme social and financial toll it would take on your family's happiness and wellbeing, you also have an obligation to protect your country from the extreme social and economic toll created by the millions of immigrants wanting to enter into our country uninvited as well.

Politicians are quick to remind the American people that we are a nation of immigrants, but they fail to make the vital distinction between what drives today's mass illegal immigration, which is welfare versus what drove the mass legal immigration from Europe to the United States during the Industrial Revolution. In the past, people were looking for freedom; now, they are looking for welfare. In 2015, Philosopher Stefan Molyneux, in his YouTube episode, *The Truth About Immigration and Welfare,* discussed a Center for Immigration Studies report titled, *"Welfare Use by Immigrant and Native Households"* which analyzed data using the Census Bureau's Survey of Income and Participation (SIPP). The report revealed that in 2012, 70% of Hispanic immigrant households received government assistance.

The Federation for American Immigration Reform estimated that illegal immigration costs the US taxpayer $113 billion a year at the federal, state, and local level. To help put this $113 billion in real perspective, Flint Michigan Mayor Karen Weaver, estimated that it would cost $1.5 billion to replace the city's toxic water pipes. Too bad our politicians elected to spend billions on subsidizing illegal immigration instead of choosing to spend that money on new water pipes for Flint residents. Now there are children in Flint with permanent disabilities because Congress and former President Obama's fiscal priorities were not in order.

Another important consideration which should cause Americans to rethink their views on supporting open borders is the fact that the US population now stands at 320 million. Comparatively, in 1900, when close to 500,000 immigrants were arriving annually to Ellis Island, the US population was only 76 million. The human race is going to have to survive on earth with finite resources for hundreds of thousands of years to come. Shouldn't Americans take measures to preserve the limited resources within the US by maintaining a stable populace? I recognize there are other countries like China and India that have much larger populations than ours, but with that said, those large populations are creating substantial environmental problems for which there are no good solutions. Is that our destiny?

Lew Rockwell once proclaimed, "Obviously, in a pure open borders system, the Western welfare states would simply be overrun by foreigners seeking tax dollars." Today, we are witnessing his forecast unfold throughout Europe. If the US continues to allow illegal immigrants to flow into our lands, the high birth rates of those population segments will cause further financial and environmental hardships here as well. Already, the Census Bureau now estimates the US population will grow by 100 million within the next forty years, due in large part to the shortsighted immigration policies of the last forty.

16 – ON THE INCOME TAX

Every election cycle, Indiana Republican Legislators hold themselves out to the public as being fiscally conservative. And as a result of this fiscal stance, conservative-minded voters have marched rank and file to the polls to cast a ballot in favor of Republican politicians. However, now in the year 2016, I believe it is time voters start analyzing the records of these Republican legislators. Voters must conclude whether the legislators are all talk or are enacting policies which bring about fiscal responsibility, which promote limited government, and which lead to lower taxes.

For example, before the 2016 primary election, we all heard the radio advertisement aired by Trey Hollingsworth stating that Republican Senator Erin Houchin voted to raise taxes six times in six months during her first year in office. The bills Hollingsworth cited were SB 177, SB 217, SB 372, HB 1485, HB 1142, and HB 1001. When I heard the news, I then researched whether Republican State Representative Steve Davisson also supported these same bills and not to my surprise Davisson voted "YEA" on each one except for HB 1485 which was recorded on the General Assembly website as an "Excused" vote.

In *Economics in One Lesson,* author Henry Hazlitt teaches that every dollar the government spends must be raised through a dollar of taxation. It's too bad our Republican Representatives have not read this lesson, for if they had, maybe they would not have allowed Indiana government spending to increase by 2.1 billion dollars in just one year. According to Ballotpedia.org, Indiana government spending went from 27.3 billion in 2014 to $29.3 billion in 2015 (a 7.1% annual spending increase).

Indiana Republican leadership is also patting itself on the back for getting the state's income tax rate down to 3.23 percent for the coming 2017 year but this percentage is actually quite high compared to the seven states which have a 0% income tax (Alaska, Florida, Nevada, South Dakota, Texas, Washington, and Wyoming).

The Indiana income tax cut will also have an insubstantial impact on the average Hoosiers pocketbook as well. In the Indianapolis Business Journal, Larry DeBoer, a professor of economics at Purdue University, claimed that a Hoosier making $50,000 a year would save about $3.50 a month due to the income tax cuts supported by our Indiana Republican legislators (Whoopty-doo). Although, when you do see your republican representatives be sure to thank them for that $3.50.

Due to the income tax, entrepreneurs are discouraged from forming new businesses, employers are discouraged from hiring more workers, and investments in new machinery as well as, technology become less frequent. Such negative results ensue because the capital that was needed for these investments to form was instead transferred to the state. In a video blog discussing the different types of taxation, CEO of Euro Pacific Capital, Peter Schiff, stated, "The income tax is probably the worst way for a government to raise money. It is the most inefficient, ineffective, intrusive tax system that you can have."

17 – ON INFLATION

The Federal Reserve is increasing the money supply substantially, resulting in a dramatic devaluation of the dollar. According to Peter Schiff, CEO of Euro Pacific Capital, Inc., the Federal Reserve is creating one trillion new dollars every year. In the article, *"The Trillion Dollar Trick,"* Schiff stated, "The Fed expands its balance sheet by buying government bonds from private banks. In exchange for these securities, the Fed credits the banks with funds it creates out of thin air. The banks then pass the funds to the general public through loans. But it's important to realize that the Fed does not have any money actually to buy the bonds in the first place. The funds are created by a fed computer." In the introduction to his book, *The Biggest Con*, Irwin Schiff, the late father of Peter Schiff, went as far as saying that the US government "runs the world's largest counterfeiting operation."

The Federal Reserve's policy of inflation allows the federal government to subsidize special interest with its newly created money, fund wars, and monetize the government debt.

Monetary inflation is a hidden tax on the public, but it is a gem to the banks, government contractors, and the federal government itself. It is a gem because when this newly created money is printed and handed out to the government and its favored recipients, the prices on goods in the marketplace have not yet adjusted upwards. For a better understanding of this practice, imagine if you were the only person in America with a printing press. Anytime you needed to pay a bill or purchase an item you could print up some more dollars. This would be a great benefit to you but now imagine that everyone had a printing press but you. Demand in the marketplace for goods and services would then far exceed the supply of products and services available. As a result, prices would skyrocket as soon as the new money began to circulate, and as a result, you, the American without the printing press, would be exposed to these higher prices. This very scenario is what is happening today, except on a less drastic scale, when the Federal Reserve increases the money supply. The government and its cronies who have the printing press at their disposal benefit from the newly created money, but you do not.

The increase of fiat currency, instead of an increase in real resources, means that a larger amount of dollars is chasing the same supply of goods, creating rising prices. You can see these rising prices most where the new government money is being spent on things such as healthcare, housing, the military, and public education.

On July 25, 2012, the House voted 327-98, on legislation to subject the Federal Reserve to an audit. Of course, this overwhelming support for a bill that would place a check on government power was nothing but a political trick. Senate Majority Leader Harry Reid vowed that the Audit by the Fed legislation would not be brought to a vote in the Senate, so the Congressional Democrats and Republicans could vote for the bill, making it appear they were voting in favor of the legislation while knowing full well that the legislation would never actually become law.

With an appreciating dollar, the American laborer would be able to steadily save his money over time, enabling him to start businesses or purchase real estate (the basis of all economic security) or invest. With time, his wealth would accumulate, he would no longer have to worry about living from paycheck to paycheck, and he would have real economic security. Yet, due to the depreciating dollar Americans are working from, "can't see in the morning," to, "can't see at night," and have nothing to show for it. The average American has no savings, no real assets of value, and as a result, no economic security. The government has siphoned off the wealth through inflation and taxation faster than Americans have been able to accumulate it, and as a result of this chronic practice of uncontrolled spending by our politicians, millions of Americans are staring economic privation in the face.

18 – ON IRAQ

In March of 2003, the United States of America waged war on the nation of Iraq. A war based on the policy of preemption: the idea that the US will attack any foreign nation that is viewed as a perceived threat. A war based on a nation's arcane but cognitive desire for Middle Eastern oil. A war based on spreading western-style democracy upon a Muslim world that has been predestined from the teachings of Muhammad to support an Islamic caliphate.

Our 43rd president deceived his supporters so they would march with him into this unnecessary battle. On January 28th, 2003, at his State of the Union address, our 43rd President stated confidently to all that would listen, that Saddam Hussein had plans to team up with the Al-Qaeda terrorist network to create a day of horror, unlike any other. He told how Saddam Hussein had 30,000 chemical weapons, how Iraq had recently sought uranium from Africa to develop a nuclear arsenal, and how the gravest danger facing America was this outlaw regime known as Iraq.

What our 43rd President failed to mention was that the United States had already become militarily involved with Iraq in the Iran-Iraq war of the 1980s by shipping weapons to the Iraqi government. This information was brought to light in US Senator Robert Byrd's book *Losing America.* Later, our strategic relations with Iraq would come to an end when, during the Iraq invasion of Kuwait, we became militarily involved in yet another Middle Eastern clash, but this time in favor of Kuwait.

Our founding fathers were supporters of non-interventionism and diplomacy. These great men understood the consequences a nation can suffer under a kingdom determined on spreading its empire across the globe. That is why the founders put the power to declare war with the legislative branch, the branch most aligned with American people, because they knew the American citizenry would be less apt to support Congressmen who support war since it is the citizenry who must fight the battles that our congressmen choose. Yet, our legislative branch continues to fund this needless war; our 44th president continues to follow blindly, the failing policies of our 43rd, and our nation continues to bear the wars' burdens.

This year's projected US deficit is 1.47 trillion dollars. How can our congressmen continue to fund a trillion-dollar war six thousand miles away and still say that they are committed to controlling the national debt? How long can we continually intervene around the world without suffering blowback here at home? How many trillions of dollars can a nation spend until it suffers an economic catastrophe?

Thousands of American soldiers are dead, thousands of Iraqi civilians are dead, thousands of hopes and dreams are dead, yet this war lives on.

19 – ON ISLAM

Sirat Rasul Allah (The Life of Muhammad), is the earliest known biography written about the Prophet Muhammad and has since been republished by the Oxford University Press. In that important text, author Ibn Ishaq discusses Muhammad's raid on the Quraysh tribe in the Battle of Badr. During the infamous battle, one of Muhammad's soldiers beheaded the nonbeliever Amr ibn Hisham and then threw Amr Hisham's head before Muhammed while shouting, "This is the head of the enemy of god." And Muhammed responded to the soldier's deed by giving praise to Allah.

In Robert Spencer's book, *The Truth about Muhammad,* we learn how Muhammad imposed his wrath on Jewish Poet Ka'b bin Al-Ashraf. Muhammad was outraged at Al-Ashraf for criticizing a group of Muslims, so Muhammad demanded that he be killed. The Arabian biographer, Ibn Sa'd, reported in his work, *Kitab Tabaqat Al-Kubra* (Book of the Major Classes), that after learning Al-Ashraf had been beheaded, Muhammad yelled, "Allahu Akbar (Allah is greatest)."

The Quran teaches that Muhammad's behavior is an excellent model of conduct (33:21) so could it be that the terrorist who executed French Satirists for mocking Islam may have drawn their inspiration from the prophet's treatment of Hisham and Al-Ashraf? Could Islamic Jihadist be motivated from the Quranic passage, "Surely the vilest of animals in Allah's sight are those who disbelieve?" (8:55)

Another passage from the Quran, mentioned in Robert Spencer's book, *The Politically Incorrect Guide to Islam,* further demonstrates Muhammad's attitude towards those who rejected Islam. Muhammad's Uncle Lahab inferred to Muhammad that he was a false prophet leading Muhammad to give this cursed reply, "The power of Abu Lahab will perish, and he will perish. His wealth and gains will not exempt him. He will be plunged in flaming fire, and his wife, the wood carrier, will have upon her neck a halter of palm-fibre"! (111:1-5)

According to Hadith literature, one of the central tenets of Islam is Jihad. Hadith 4645 states, "There is another act which elevates the position of a man in Paradise to a grade one hundred (higher), and the elevation between one grade and the other is equal to the height of the heaven from the earth. He (Abu Sa'id) said: "What is that act?"

He (Muhammad) replied: "Jihad in the way of Allah! Jihad in the way of Allah!"

Muhammad was able to entice his future martyrs to commit jihad by promising them rivers of milk, wine, and honey (Quran 47:15), an abundance of fruit (43:71, 73), golden thrones (Quran 56:15) and virgins (Qur'an 56:36). Even one thousand four hundred years after Muhammad's death, it was alleged that 911 hijacker Muhammad Atta decided to pack a wedding suit in his luggage because he was motivated by Muhammad's paradisiacal promises.

In fear of sounding Islamophobic, the left has refused to acknowledge what motivates Muslims to commit honor killings, to engage in holy wars, to take child brides, to punish apostasy, to force women to wear burkas and to continue to practice beheadings deep into the 21st century. These atrocities have plagued Islamic civilizations since its founding. And these atrocities will continue until people of all faiths as well as politics, join together in denouncing these horrendous, archaic Islamic practices and teachings. Muslims have committed these actions because they are actions that Muhammad committed himself, but that should not be an excuse for such actions to continue in the 21st century.

20 – ON LIBYA

Since the United States entered WW1, marking the end of the golden age of America, a period that had been in a state of relative peace since the Civil War, the US has continually involved itself in perpetual Middle Eastern state and religious conflicts. As justification for the interventions, the neoconservatives regularly cite their vision of spreading democracy to the suppressed masses. Today our government spends over a trillion dollars a year funding our military, spread out across the globe in over 130 nations. No longer does the United States abide by the traditional, foreign policy principles advocated by our founding fathers of self-determination, diplomacy, and non-interventionism. Instead, our politicians pursue a foreign policy of nation-building, pre-emptive war, and interventionism.

Thomas Jefferson once declared, "We wish not to meddle with the internal affairs of any country." If Mr. Jefferson were alive today, he would be disheartened by America's present leadership, which no longer seeks his informed counsel.

In the International Tribune of London, President Barack Obama along with UK Prime Minister David Cameron and French President Nicolas Sarkozy authored an op-ed backing action in Libya. President Barack Obama promises a low-key role in the Libyan War, but if history plays any role in this story of military intervention, further escalation of US financial and troop support seems like a forthcoming plot. Already the US has engaged in acts of war by supplying arms to the rebels and imposing sanctions on Libya.

Engaging in acts of war almost always have unintended consequences leading to further escalation. In the 1990s, our no-fly zone and trade sanctions the United States imposed on Iraq increased hostility and led the Iraqi citizenry to become more dependent upon the rule of Saddam Hussein. In 1996, after five years of Iraq sanctions, CBS reporter Lesley Stahl asked the United States Ambassador to the UN Madeleine Albright: "We have heard that half a million children have died in Iraq. Is the price worth it?"

Mrs. Albright callously replied: "We think the price is worth it."

Texas Congressman Ron Paul has given speeches on how US involvement in the Afghan-Soviet War has now come back to haunt us. In the 1980s the United States linked with Afghanistan's Mujahideen, a group which had ties with Osama Bin Laden. Our CIA supplied the

Mujahideen with weapons and provided the group training to stifle the Soviet invasion of Afghanistan.

The price is not worth it! Our interventions around the world have only led to more spending, borrowing, taxing, and conflicts. In the book, *For a New Liberty,* Economist Murray Rothbard wrote, "In the name of combating 'aggression' everywhere—of being the world's 'policeman'—it has itself become the great and permanent aggressor."

21 – ON THE MAINSTREAM MEDIA

During the third presidential debate, the left went into full meltdown mode after Donald Trump suggested that he may not accept the results of the election. The Huffington Post promptly lambasted Trump, arguing such an act would undermine American Democracy, trigger violence, and make it harder for Hillary Clinton to govern effectively. Politico remarked that such defiance by Trump would delegitimize America's electoral process. The New York Times responded to Trump's claim with a column directing him to honor the will of the American voter. And the Washington Post Editorial Board argued that such an abstention by Trump could ultimately interfere with the peaceful transition of power.

Though, now that the Democrats have lost the presidency, I fear they have all but forgotten just how important it was to them that the losing side acknowledge defeat. For example, since the election, the tolerant liberal Rosie O'Donnell has advocated for the imposition of martial law to stop our 45th President from assuming office. Does Rosie not see how her rhetoric could undermine American Democracy, trigger violence, and make it harder for Trump to govern effectively? Or look at the example set by Democratic Congressman John Lewis. He remarked that Donald Trump is not a legitimately elected US President. Surely, Congressman Lewis must recognize that he is delegitimizing America's electoral process with such a statement. Or how about CNN Commentator Van Jones labeling Donald Trump's victory as "whitelash." And believe me when I say that this statement by Van Jones was in no way meant to honor the will of the American voter.

Since Trump was the victor in the presidential election, it seems the left is no longer particularly concerned about the losing side conceding defeat like they were just before the 2016 Presidential election. Then again, I'm sure it's just a "huge" coincidence that the left abruptly stopped arguing about the importance of conceding defeat and allowing for a peaceful transition of power once the results came in, and the left realized they were on the conceding side. Sad!

22 – ON THE MINIMUM WAGE

While addressing the media in the White House, President Obama stated, “Now, it was one year ago today that I first asked Congress to raise the federal minimum wage—a federal minimum wage that in real terms is worth about 20 percent less than it was when Ronald Reagan took office.” Obama further iterated, “when Congress refuses to raise it; it loses value—because there’s a little bit inflation, everything else starts costing a little bit more.”

I wish I could challenge Obama on what entity is responsible for creating inflation, which has reduced the purchasing power of Americans. In the PBS television series, *Free to Choose*, Milton Friedman taught, “The truth is inflation is made in one place and one place only—here in Washington. This is the only place where there are presses like this that turn out these pieces of paper called money. This is the place where the power resides to determine how rapidly the amount of money shall increase.”

On the Federal Reserve website, it states that the Federal Open Market Committee has a 2 percent inflation objective, in part, to promote maximum employment. The Fed can achieve this objective by effectively lowering the cost of labor through inflation. As Financial Broker Peter Schiff explained in a column, "Put simply: because inflation reduces wages in real terms, employers can afford to hire more people." So, I find it quite hypocritical to see President Obama supporting an increase in the minimum wage, while at the same time supporting the Fed's inflationary policies which drive up prices in the economy, thereby lowering real wages for the wage earner.

In *Choice,* Robert Murphy, who holds a Ph.D. in economics from New York University, wrote, "...if other interventions have artificially raised wage rates and the other implicit costs of employment, institutional unemployment results. Rather than admitting the folly of these original interventions, another possible remedy is to inflate the currency, thereby raising prices in general and effectively reducing the real wage rate. In other words, rather than asking unions to go along with lower nominal wages in order to restore full employment, the government can simply create more price inflation to make workers effectively poorer without it being obvious."

For decades, politicians have advocated for increases in the minimum wage, while at the same time, those very politicians support the federal government's inflationary policies which more than offset any minimum wage increase they vote for.

But simply raising the minimum wage higher is not the answer either since such policy, in effect, outlaws employment for those low-skilled laborers whose productivity is below the minimum wage threshold. In *Planning for Freedom,* Ludwig von Mises, who holds a doctorate in law and economics from the University of Vienna, wrote, "The only means to raise wage rates permanently for all those eager to earn wages is to raise the productivity of labor by increasing the per-head quota of capital invested and improving the methods of production."

23 – ON POLITICAL PARTIES

"Keep your eye on one thing, and one thing only: how much government is spending because that's the true tax ... If you're not paying for it in the form of explicit taxes, you're paying for it indirectly in the form of inflation or in the form of borrowing."

These are the words of free-market economist Milton Friedman. Friedman was a man who thought for himself and saw through the propaganda of both parties and, as a result, was able to give impartial, insightful analysis in his books as well as in his speeches, about the economic harms caused by the policies of the left and right.

Over the last two presidencies', a large portion of society has become indoctrinated instead of educated through television media outlets like Fox News, CNN, or MSNBC. We see this indoctrination when conservative voters cheerily support Republican candidates who have only given lip service to the ideas of limited government. Every election season these "so-called" fiscal conservatives make a reappearance into communities promising that, if elected, they will cut taxes and restrain government, but when election season is over, these statements transform into empty promises.

Milton Friedman teaches that the actual burden of taxation is what government spends. Therefore, the only way to decrease taxation is by abolishing or reducing the cost of government programs, agency budgets, state salaries, and overall government interventions within the economy. If our fellow Republican voters took the time to educate themselves on the issues, they would learn that the politicians they blindly support never reduce spending. When politicians claim they cut spending, what they mean is that they decreased the projected rate of increase in government spending. Under George W. Bush, the federal budget increased by trillions. Under the Indiana Republican administrations of Mitch Daniels and Mike Pence, the Indiana state budget has increased by billions.

To our fellow Democrat voters, I urge the same message: The citizen must correct the economic mistruths that are continually spread by the ill-informed Democratic brass. Friedman and other like-minded men have destroyed the modern, liberal arguments for a large central government by demonstrating how democratic policies have led to skyrocketing debts, a dwindling manufacturing sector, unbridled illegal immigration, a class of people that are dependent on government assistance, and a federal government dependent on foreign capital, high taxes, and a printing press.

In 1800, Thomas Jefferson was elected to the presidency on a classical liberal democrat platform which endorsed peace, a strict adherence to the Constitution, state sovereignty, freedom of religion, government frugality, and capitalism. Today, the definition of liberal shares no resemblance to the classical term; a development that must be reversed.

The Democrat and Republican Parties are special-interest groups designed to obtain privileges for the factions they represent at the expense of those they don't. This two-party monopoly has plundered Americans of their savings and wealth. As Americans, we must stand above party politics by relentlessly opposing their anointed puppets. And we must start supporting those who possess the principles and competence to hold such high offices.

24 – ON PRESIDENT TRUMP'S IMMIGRATION BAN

Currently, ISIS is taking advantage of our western government's generosity towards refugees to infiltrate the United States and Europe. Speaking exclusively to BuzzFeed, an Operative of ISIS revealed that the terror group had infiltrated the droves of refugees flowing into Western lands. Former CIA Director John Brennan along with NATO Commander Philip Breedlove has since substantiated such claims.

Senator Jeff Sessions has tabulated a list of 19 Refugees and one Iraqi Special Immigration Visa recipient who have been associated with terrorism, yet the left is completely disregarding this information. Members of the left would rather risk seeing innocent Americans getting killed by an Islamic terrorist than risk the chance that they will be labeled a racist or Islamophobe by their leftist brethren.

In 2011, Barack Obama stopped processing Iraq refugees for six months, but I don't recall the left protesting en masse over the actions taken by Obama then nor do I recall the left protesting en masse over the 26,171 bombs Obama dropped on predominantly Muslim countries in 2016. Likewise, Obama's interventionist foreign policy in Syria and Libya helped facilitate the current refugee crisis, so where was the left's moral outrage when he and Secretary Clinton were intervening in those countries?

Immigrant Tashfeen Malik, who killed 14 people and injured 22 others in San Bernardino, California, was born in Pakistan. Omar Mateen, whose parents emigrated to the US from Afghanistan, killed 49 people and severely injured 49 more. Somali Refugee, Abdul Ali Artan drove a car into a crowd of students at Ohio State University wounding 11. These are the grisly episodes that President Trump is trying to stop with proper vetting. Today, there are Americans permanently maimed, who are forever confined to a wheelchair, their injuries forcing them to live in a reclusive state, every waking moment they suffer mentally, their lives now all but destroyed due to the left's "generous" immigration policies. How is Donald Trump evil for trying to put an end to such wrongs? According to the Center for Immigration Studies, it costs $12,874 to promptly resettle a refugee in the US, but only $1,057 to resettle a refugee in the Middle East. Therefore, the most cost-effective use of tax dollars would be to finance the relocation of refugees within Middle Eastern territories, enabling America to help a vastly greater number of refugees than what otherwise would be obtainable through relocations within the US.

The more we intervene in the Mid-East, the more radical Islamists we import to the United States, and the more probable it is we will suffer terrorist attacks. British Journalist Milo Yiannopoulos recently remarked, "Every country deserves to have control of its border, and decide who is allowed to immigrate. Wanting this doesn't make you racist, evil, or even particularly conservative." Yes, and Milo is right. I just wish the left could recognize it.

25 – ON PUBLIC UNIVERSITY ADMISSIONS

Today, 61% of students from the 2012-2013 IU Maurer School of Law 1L class are not from Indiana. In contrasts, the University of Kentucky College of Law 1L law class is only 30% out of state. And every year, the IU Mauer School of Law registers 65 to 75 graduate students who come from more than 25 nations.

Such IU recruiting policies have not just occurred at the law school but throughout the entire IU system. Schools across the country recruit out-of-state students for financial reasons, but it would be a better policy for Indiana, and every other state, to recruit more of its citizens such as the UK College of Law does, so students won't have to be bombarded with out-of-state tuition rates and debt because they couldn't get accepted into the school of their home state. Students across Indiana are being shut out from public university programs their families worked so hard to pay for with their tax dollars. I am a living witness to this disheartening situation even within my community. Fortunately, I was accepted into my desired IU program, but had I been denied, it would have been a financial hardship for my family to send me out of state.

Our so-called university intellectuals' like to raise the benevolent talking point that recruiting international students promotes diversity. However, these individuals of power will tell you only that which will benefit themselves. The out-of-state student tuition fee at the IU Maurer School of Law is $45,602 a year, whereas, the in-state student tuition fee is $28,130 so there is a financial incentive for IU to recruit out of state students. Although, this talking point might strike a nerve with the public, so the officials hide this increased revenue generation under the cloak of "promoting diversity."

Already, IUB has over 6,000 international students receiving educations, so they can one day own and operate the businesses that Indianans will be forced to work for or compete against.

In the *Autobiography of Malcolm X*, Malcolm, after reforming himself into a great leader, came back to the Harlem ghetto to visit an old acquaintance named West Indian Archie. Archie had a great mathematical mind. From his photographic memory, he could mentally record hundreds of number combinations a day, but Archie never made it out of the ghetto. Malcolm X was bitter because he knew Archie could have been a great mathematician or engineer, but instead, Archie was a dying criminal, decrepit from drug addiction. And I know individuals from my community, with great minds, who, if they had lived in a society with a sense of commitment towards its people, their talents might have been better utilized as well.

26 – ON REFUGEE RESETTLEMENT

President Obama is still adamant in relocating thousands of Syrian refugees into the United States, even after it was revealed that one of the Paris terrorists entered Europe from allegedly claiming to be a Syrian war refugee.

But due to President Obama's inability to accept the truth about the dangers that lurk in allowing thousands of alleged Syrian refugees into the US after fifteen years of persistent US military interventions in the Middle East, thirty governors have stood up for American interest and opposed the idea of Syrian resettlement in their respective states.

Allowing thousands of Syrian refugees into the US would cause a sundry of negative side effects for our country. Such policy would enable the federal government to justify the further militarization of the police, to broaden the already intrusive federal surveillance programs in the name of national security, and to warrant more military actions overseas, when America suffers yet another Islamic terrorist attack here at home. Senior Research Fellow at the Heritage Foundation, Robert Rector, estimated it would cost 6.5 billion dollars to resettle 10,000 refugees in America during their lifespans. Of course, the majority of Americans who champion mass subsidized refugee resettlement as a benevolent cause have yet to make a single donation to a refugee and are instead, expecting the poor taxpayer to make the financial contribution on their behalf.

Since the attacks, FBI Director James Comey and the chairman of the House of Homeland Security Committee, Mike McCaul, have both noted that there are gaping holes in the vetting process. At a September security conference, Director of National Intelligence, James Clapper, stated: “I don’t, obviously, put it past the likes of ISIL to infiltrate operatives among these refugees, so that’s a huge concern of ours." Syrian Ambassador to India, Riad Abbas, substantiated Clapper’s fears, by stating, “Among the refugees, who went to Europe, maybe more than 20 percent belong to ISIL groups.” So, I challenge those who support resettlement to combat these revelations with arguments, instead of merely shouting the censoring words “Islamophobe” and “xenophobe.”

Self-preservation is an instinct that supports survival. Millions of years of evolutionary progress have enabled species to develop mechanisms that detect threats from other organisms. An animal raised in the wild can utilize such survival skills to protect itself from apparent danger, whereas, if an animal is raised in captivity but is later released into the wild it cannot utilize such skills because its instincts have weakened. Could it be some Americans support resettlement only because they have lived their entire lives in a captive state, free from the perils that are rooted within the nature of Islamic cultures?

Author and founder of the Ludwig von Mises Institute, Lew Rockwell, in a speech, explained how politically enforced multiculturalism has been quite harmful to modern civilization. Rockwell remarked, "Whether it's Czechoslovakia, Yugoslavia, the Soviet Union, or Pakistan and Bangladesh, or Malaysia and Singapore, or the countless places with ethnic and religious divides that have not yet been resolved to this day, the evidence suggests something rather different from the tale of universal brotherhood that is such a staple of leftist folklore."

27 – ON SAVING

When turning on your television to watch the evening news this holiday season, you likely saw hordes of shoppers picking out gifts and swiping their credit cards with their shopping carts filled. According to the American Research Group, the average American was expected to spend $984 on gifts this Christmas.

Meanwhile, the Bureau of Economic Analysis reported a US household savings rate of only 3.1% for October 2017. This rate is likely even lower now that we're in the holiday season. Due to the high amount of spending on gifts this Christmas, retail sales are expected to surpass $1 trillion, as they did in 2016. But are such spending habits good for the US economy?

First, these images depict consumers racking up credit card debt. Accumulating debt to purchase gifts or any other unnecessary goods is not a wise financial decision. These consumers will not only have to pay the credit card principal but also the interest. This extra expense due to interest payments ultimately causes a reduction in the capacity for consumption in the future.

The money consumers now have to spend on interest payments is money they otherwise could have been free to spend on something else.

When American buyers borrow to consume, they acquire no income-producing asset. Then, when it becomes time to pay back borrowed funds, these consumers must dip into their savings. This phenomenon contrasts with the borrowing of entrepreneurs, investors, and companies who put the funds of individual savers towards productive efforts, such as installing a more efficient machine or investing in innovative technologies.

These investments increase the productive capacity of the US economy, leading to higher wages, lower prices, and increased profits. As author Robert Murphy explains in *Lessons for the Young Economist*, "If the savings are channeled into expanding production (rather than merely financing consumption), then 'total output' grows over time…"

How would retail businesses fare by such a change in the spending habits of the American consumer? Regarding this question, Robert Murphy explained, "These large swings in how people spent their incomes—diverting it away from consumption and towards investment—would ultimately steer workers and other resources out of industries catering to immediate consumption, and toward industries catering to long-range production."

Avoiding the burdens of credit card debt and improving the productive capacity of the US economy may very well be enough incentive for consumers to save, but savings introduces many other benefits. For example, saving creates a rainy day fund, ensuring consumers against future misfortune; it allows one to receive the satisfaction of watching his or her bank account grow; it increases the threshold for future spending plans; it allows for greater independence, and it generates the ability to transfer more resources to loved ones.

Saving is a discipline requiring great self-control, but the rewards that accompany such discipline are ample. Please keep that in mind this Christmas.

28 – ON SLAVERY

Daily, I watch the mainstream media and left-leaning politicians play the race card at every opportunity. They incessantly associate America's citizenry, heritage, and culture with slavery and racism. Today, more than ever, the left links patriotic Americans to white nationalism and the KKK. Liberals deploy this scare tactic to assassinate the characters of the politicians and constituencies who are not promoting their leftist ideology.

Every race has owned slaves. In the book *Black Rednecks and White Liberals*, African American author and economist Thomas Sowell wrote, "Even at the peak of the Atlantic slave trade, Africans retained more slaves for themselves than they sent to the Western Hemisphere." On Politifact.com, the University of North Carolina historian, Joseph T. Glatthaar, estimated that in the year 1860, less than five percent of American citizens in slave-owning states owned slaves. Although if someone conducted a poll today, I imagine it would indicate that the average American mistakenly believes that percentage to be closer to 100%, since there is a class of people who, "make a business of keeping the troubles, the wrongs, and the hardships of the [black] race before the public...", as Booker T. Washington once observed.

Dr. Peter Hammond provided an excellent account of the prevalence of slavery among other civilizations and religions in his book, *Slavery, Terrorism, and Islam*. For example, according to Dr. Hammond, the Islamic slave trade lasted over fourteen centuries, and the entire enterprise caused far greater death than the North Atlantic slave trade, which lasted just over three centuries. Dr. Hammond noted how the Islamic slave trade is one of history's "best-kept secrets." A secret, which sadly, has led to a lack of perspective among the American public about slavery's global past. Many Americans feel resentment and anger towards the United States because of their lack of education and knowledge about how systematic slavery was throughout the world. In reality, America has done more for the cause of freedom than any other country on this earth.

In Chapter 1, Dr. Hammond stated, "Muhammad himself owned many slaves, some of whom he captured in wars of conquest and some he purchased." Hammond taught how "North African Muslim pirates abducted and enslaved more than 1 million Europeans between 1530 and 1780." Later in Chapter 7, Dr. Hammond noted that India's western region was named Hindu Kush (the slaughter of the Hindu) to remind the Hindus of the vast number of slaves who perished crossing the Afghan Mountains to the Muslim markets in Central Asia. Such history demonstrates that slave ownership is in no way peculiar to the United States or to white skin.

The British Parliament outlawed slavery across its empire in 1833; the United States officially ended slavery in 1865 by passing the 13th amendment. Not all countries were so quick to experience such enlightened thinking though, considering that slavery existed in Ethiopia until 1942, in Saudi Arabia until 1962, and in India until 1976, according to Dr. Hammond.

Walter Williams of George Mason University pointed out that "The most unique aspect of slavery in the Western world was the moral outrage against it, which began to emerge in the 18th century and led to massive elimination efforts." Williams went on, "It was Britain's military sea power that put an end to the slave trade. And our country fought a costly war that brought an end to slavery. Unfortunately, these facts about slavery are not in the lessons taught in our schools and colleges. Instead, there is a gross misrepresentation and suggestion that slavery was a uniquely American practice."

29 – ON SOCIALISM

In the 2016 primary, sadly over thirteen million Americans supported a socialist for President of the United States, so I wanted to take this time to explain why socialism is unworthy of American support.

In his latest book, *The Problem with Socialism*, Thomas DiLorenzo, an economics professor at Loyola University, described why socialism is an unworkable economic system due to three fundamental problems.

One such problem stems from incentives. For instance, while private ownership incentivizes responsible stewardship, no such incentives derive from large scale common ownership. Take, for example, the islands of socialism within inner cities, there, we see governmental housing quickly turn dilapidated because the occupants have no financial incentive to maintain or improve the property. DiLorenzo illustrated another example of the incentive problem with his discussion of the Soviet Union's exploitation of the Black Sea:

> To meet government issued five-year plans for housing and other construction, builders extracted gravel and sand from around Black Sea beaches (and knocked down a lot of trees to do so). Because there was no private property, no value was attached to the gravel, or to the trees, or to the shoreline. Because the gravel was "free," contractors hauled away as much as possible—before someone else did.

Socialism also has a knowledge problem. In capitalist societies, there are millions of investors, entrepreneurs, and laborers who possess unique information and skills. Skills that enable them to create the products and provide the services that the billions of consumers demand. In an economy run by government planners, the vast array of knowledge required to meet such needs cannot exist. The small number of government planners cannot possibly possess all the information necessary to operate a complex economy efficiently.

For example, think of a $15 an hour minimum wage set by a government official. Now think of a grocery store owner who manages his small grocery every day, who knows all the ins and outs of his grocery business. Who do you think possesses the most knowledge on what a proper wage rate would be for those grocery employees? Who do you think would have the most information to decide what wages would work, to allow for profits versus not work? The government official who knows nothing about that grocery store operation or the grocery store owner who manages the store every day?

Socialism also has a calculation problem. In a 2016 column featured on LewRockwell.com, Economist Dominick T. Armentano, explained how under socialism "...where the crucial factors of production (such as capital and land) are owned by the State, there are no meaningful price signals or profit and loss incentives to ensure that scarce resources are used efficiently and not wasted." As a result, central planners aren't able to "...decide which factor combinations are the cheapest or which outputs and investments would tend to maximize consumer welfare."

A graduate of Harvard and Columbia, Thomas Woods, in his book, *The Church and the Market*, summarized the problem as follows, "Now prices emerge as a result of the ongoing interaction of buyers and sellers, each exchanging his private property. But if the state owns all the means of production, no such exchange takes place, and the process that gives rise to prices in a capitalist system, therefore, simply does not exist. So without private ownership of the means of production, there can be no prices for capital goods, and without such prices, the socialist planning board must grope in the dark in its allocation of capital."

In his book, *Socialism: An Economic and Sociological Analysis*, Economist Ludwig von Mises warned, "It is not the pioneer of a better and finer world, but the spoiler of what thousands of years of civilization have created. It does not build; it destroys. For destruction is the essence of it. It produces nothing, it only consumes what the social order based on private ownership in the means of production has created."

30 – ON STATE NULLIFICATION

After Kentucky Clerk Kim Davis' refusal to issue a marriage license to a gay couple, there was a lot of anger directed at her for not abiding by the US Supreme Court's edict on the issue. The problem with this argument is that the US Supreme Court's ruling in *Obergefell v. Hodges* was wrong. Under the 10th amendment of the US Constitution, the US Supreme Court should not have the authority to override the Kentucky Constitution on the issue of marriage licenses. Under the 10th amendment, all powers not explicitly delegated to the federal government belong to the states. So, Mrs. Davis was correctly abiding by the Kentucky Constitution when she refused to issue the marriage license to the gay couple since the Kentucky Constitution defines marriage as being between a man and a woman. Whether she knew it or not, Kim Davis was engaging in nullification.

Current Chief Justice Roberts acknowledged that the Supreme Court lacked the authority to hear the case. His *Obergefell* dissent read, "This court is not a legislature. Whether same-sex marriage is a good idea should be of no concern to us." He went on, "If you are among the many Americans—of whatever sexual orientation—who favor expanding same-sex marriage, by all means, celebrate today's decision...But do not celebrate the Constitution. It had nothing to do with it."

The founding fathers understood that it would be the nature of the federal government to usurp the rights of the state governments. To protect the states from such foreseeable federal usurps, the founders ratified the tenth amendment which assures that the limited powers each state delegated to the federal government could not be expanded upon except through the amendment process. Article 1 Section 8 lines out the powers delegated to the federal congress by the states, and marriage licensing is not listed.

In the book, *Nullification: How to Resist Federal Tyranny in the 21st Century,* author Tom Woods writes, "When the Constitution was ratified, the people were assured that it established a government of limited powers (primarily related to foreign policy and regulation of interstate commerce), that the states retained all powers not delegated to the new government, and that the federal government could exercise no additional powers without their consent, given in the form of constitutional amendments."

Nullification has been utilized by our state governments several times throughout history. For example, Jefferson used nullification to help bring an end to the Alien and Sedition Acts. The Supreme Court of Wisconsin declared the Fugitive Slave Act unconstitutional and thereby voided by citing Jefferson's Kentucky Resolution of 1798. Some argue that Nullification violates the Supremacy Clause of the Constitution, but those who make such claims are deleting significant text from the clause. Jefferson was fully aware of the complete phrase and reminded his friends that only the laws made "in pursuance" of the Constitution should have supremacy. And in regard to the Equal Protection Clause argument, Harvard Professor Raoul Berger's book, *Government by Judiciary: The Transformation of the Fourteenth Amendment*, proves through meticulous constitutional scholarship that the purpose of Sec. 1 of the 14th Amendment was to extend citizenship to freed slaves and to guard them against Black Codes.

Kentucky's US Senator Rand Paul exhibited his keen understanding of the Jeffersonian state rights tradition when he told CNN, during an interview about the jailing of Kentucky Clerk Kim Davis, that "the federal government should not get involved in something that has always been a local issue."

31 – ON SUBSIDIES

"The people that once bestowed commands, consulships, legions, and all else, now meddles no more and longs eagerly for just two things—bread and circuses." This quote is from the Roman satirist Juvenal. I find his words relevant today as Indiana's politicians and a portion of our public salivate at the thought of building yet another tax-subsidized sports stadium. During the reign of Emperor Claudius, it was written that the Roman Empire had 159 holidays, of which 93 were for games. These state-sponsored spectacles acted as a narcotic for the public, taking up their time and diverting their passions, so the masses would be too sidetracked to advocate against the unwarranted taxes and mounting debts their political leaders were subjecting them to.

The public financing of entertainment became so prevalent, author Jerome Carcopino, in his book *Daily Life in Ancient Rome*, wrote, "In order to put an end to corrupt practices, the Senate in 63 B.C. passed a law disqualifying for election any magistrate who had financed such shows for the two years preceding the voting."

Currently, we have politicians blurting out conventional mantras to justify the stadiums' construction on the public dime. They claim, “it will increase jobs,” or that, “it will stimulate the economy,” but the problem is when you go back and look at similar cases, the benefits aren’t there. In reality, the profits will only go towards a privileged few like owner Ersal Ozdemir, the construction contractors, and players. This small group of individuals has an enormously strong financial interest in seeing the stadium’s completion, but there is not any comparable group that has enough financial interest to form an opposition since the cost will be spread out among many taxpayers. Our only hope it seems is that our legislature remembers that for every dollar taken away from the taxpayer is a dollar the taxpayer could have spent on his or her most urgent needs.

Many US politicians claim they are supporters of the free market, but their actions speak otherwise. In a free market, private investors have to be careful when investing their funds because if they make a bad loan, they lose their investment. Whereas, if a bureaucrat makes a bad loan, the bureaucrat loses nothing, only the taxpayer suffers. During the 1900s after a series of public-private partnership failures, Indiana, Ohio, and Illinois all amended their constitutions to prohibit government subsidies to private corporations, but now states are getting around these constitutional restrictions by modern-day financing schemes and an all too accommodating legislature.

Entrepreneur James Hill built a transcontinental railroad without being subsidized by the state. So yes, it's feasible that Mr. Ozdemir's venture can be funded with today's modern financial markets. Ultimately, no matter how the stadium is constructed, it will be built by private capital. Though, if the politicians have it their way, it will be built with private capital that has been confiscated from the citizens versus capital voluntarily put up by investors.

There are several economic reasons why the state should not subsidize sports stadiums:

First, when consumers spend money at the stadium, they will have less money to spend on local businesses within the community like restaurants and theaters. In his classic book, *Economics in One Lesson,* Henry Hazlitt teaches us, "All that has happened, at best, is that there has been a diversion of jobs because of the project." We are merely taking money from the left hand and putting it in the right.

Secondly, the politicians and owners almost always underestimate the costs and overestimate the benefits. After the Beijing Olympics, the famous Bird's Nest Stadium became nothing but an empty and costly relic.

Thirdly, government spending discourages investments. After subsidizing the University of Phoenix Stadium and several other sports arenas, the city of Glendale, Arizona, has resulted to increasing taxes and cutting public services so it can attempt to service its $25-million-a-year debt. Because of poor decisions like those being made by public officials in Glendale, private capital is being taxed away before it can be accumulated across America. These high taxes will delay investments in new machinery, deter individuals from starting new businesses, and cause companies to be wary of expanding or taking on more employees.

The state should be frugal, thereby creating an environment where Hoosiers can build up their individual savings. Private savings enable investments to occur in the economy, allowing for higher productivity. Capital accumulation, coupled with innovative minds, are the true engines of economic growth.

32 – ON SYRIA

Amnesty International released a report in late 2015 that found the terrorist group ISIS is equipped with US weapons, which were seized from Syrian rebels and the Iraqi Army. After reviewing similar findings, Former Congressman Ron Paul, in the article, *Paris and What Should Be Done,* wrote, "Because the US and its allies are essentially on the same side as ISIS and other groups—seeking the overthrow of Assad—many of the weapons they have sent to the more "moderate" factions also seeking Assad's ouster have ended up in the hands of radicals." The honorable Congressman went on to ask, "Does anyone not believe this is a recipe for the kind of disaster we have now seen in Paris? The French, in particular, have been very active in arming even the more radical groups in Syria, as they push for more political influence in the region. Why do they still refuse to believe in the concept of blowback?"

In January 2002, after discussing the wrongs committed by Saddam, Senator Obama professed, "But I also know that Saddam poses no imminent and direct threat to the United States or to his neighbors, that the Iraqi economy is in shambles, that the Iraqi military is a fraction of its former strength, and that in concert with the international community he can be contained until, in the way of all petty dictators, he falls away into the dustbin of history." Now in the year 2016, could Obama not have taken that same 2002 address, and inserted the name Assad in place of the name Saddam and inserted the name Syria in place of the name Iraq and still reach the same conclusion not to intervene?

In that same address, Senator Obama claimed that the Iraq War was not based on "reason but on passion, not on principle but on politics." And now as we fast forward to 2016, the President and his coalition partners Turkey and Saudi Arabia are preparing to supply more weapons to rebels in Syria to counter the Russian-backed Assad regime. Was this policy decision not based on politics?

In 1961, Dwight Eisenhower warned, "In the councils of government, we must guard against the acquisition of unwarranted influence, whether sought or unsought, by the military-industrial complex." Since taking office, our Nobel Peace Prize Laureate has bombed Afghanistan, Iraq, Pakistan, Somalia, Yemen, Libya, and Syria. Clearly, Obama's been influenced, and I hope his military blunders serve as a lesson to future peace candidates to surround themselves with peace-minded councils that will help provide a formidable defense against those who will come calling for war.

The Syrian War has allegedly caused over 470,000 deaths, and for what? As citizens, we must reject our current interventionist foreign policy. We must reject regime change and refuse the constant shipping of arms to the Middle East. If the US would garnish peace through diplomacy, trade, and respecting the sovereignty of foreign nations, the world may soon emulate, civility may foster, and with time the hatred directed towards the west may cool.

33 – ON TAXATION

The State of Illinois recently increased the income tax rate by 32%, even though it already has some of the highest property taxes in the country. Due to these increases, it's reported that an additional $5 billion will be confiscated from Illinois citizens and diverted to the state. This year in Indiana, the Republican-led legislature increased 45 different taxes and fees, which included a considerable tax hike on gasoline. Government's appetite for tax dollars has and will continue to hamper private enterprise and destroy the ability of Americans to save.

In his eye-opening work, *The Biggest Con*, investor Irwin Schiff asserts that capital accumulation distinguishes an advancing economy from a stagnant one, and the destruction of capital by a government causes economies to falter. Similarly, in his grand treatise, *Human Action*, Ludwig von Mises contends, "If taxes grow beyond a moderate limit, they cease to be taxes and turn into devices for the destruction of the market economy." Across the United States, we have witnessed this destruction. The state has dissipated the savings necessary for

Americans to draw upon to build businesses, factories, and machinery.

Without savings, investment cannot take place, and the wealth that would have been created from those investments will not come into existence. Excessive taxation redirects resources away from businesses that would have used those resources to improve the productivity of their plants, the efficiency of their labor force, and the sophistication of their products. Excessive taxation hinders the ability of companies to compete and expand, causing the US to have a weaker and less robust economy.

At one time, private capital was directed into manufacturing powerhouses like Detroit, Gary, and Akron, creating further industry, employment, and helping America create the world's largest trade surplus. The government has now seized such capital and allocated it to favored political constituencies. One consequence of the government's appetite for private sector earnings is that numerous US manufacturers have now opted to relocate in less restrictive markets overseas. Excessive taxation and regulation have perpetuated the offshoring of American industry, and in a few short decades has quickly transformed a record-breaking trade surplus into a record-breaking trade deficit.

Besides providing benefits to the economy, spending also needs to be cut so that Americans won't become dependent upon the state. In *Back on the Road to Serfdom*, historian Tom Woods cautioned, "All over the world, the impossible promises governments have made to their populations are beginning to unravel. Millions of people have arranged their lives in the expectation of various forms of government support that will be mathematically impossible to provide."

It's not government bureaucrats who create wealth. Wealth comes from the millions of Americans making products. Wealth stems from profits, which sends signals on where to allocate scarce resources most efficiently. Wealth is created by increasing worker output. It's built from savings, accurate forecasts, investments, and production within the market economy.

34 – ON THOMAS JEFFERSON

The Indiana Democratic Party's annual Jefferson-Jackson Day Dinner taking place June 17th has been renamed the Hoosier Hospitality Dinner to appease a small noisy faction of leftists. In reality, I don't mind the name change since the classical liberal principles Thomas Jefferson once so eloquently advocated for are no longer practiced by the Democrats. But little did the Democrats who supported this name change know that their unwavering appeasement towards minute factions of the party has often angered and disenfranchised much larger factions of the party base.

Thomas Jefferson was known to study for fifteen hours a day. He was an avid reader of John Locke, Adam Smith, Antoine Destutt de Tracy, Francis Bacon, and Isaac Newton—to name a few. At the age of twenty-six, Jefferson designed his Monticello home. Jefferson founded the University of Virginia, he wrote the Virginia statute for religious freedom, was a Minister to France, Governor of Virginia, and arguably our greatest President.

Thomas Jefferson helped free millions of individuals from the tyranny of the British Crown. Does not such an act deserve praise and commemoration? Americans must acknowledge that Jefferson's contributions to the human race far outweigh any subtraction.

In the Declaration of Independence, Jefferson wrote the legendary words, "all men are created equal." Martin Luther King has cited this immortal phrase. Ho Chi Minh recited this phrase on September 2, 1945, when Vietnam declared independence from France. As Barack Obama recently stated of Jefferson's phrase, "It inspired movements around the world."

Jefferson was a fierce advocate for freedom of speech. When the Adams administration passed the Sedition Act, it restricted particular speech critical of the government and its officials. Jefferson was appalled at this encroachment upon the First Amendment. He immediately drafted the Kentucky Resolve which supported state nullification of the act, and once elected president, Jefferson no longer enforced the unconstitutional legislation.

In *Free to Choose*, Milton Friedman wrote that Jefferson, "agonized repeatedly about slavery, suggested in his notes and correspondence plans for eliminating slavery, but never publicly proposed any such plans..." In truth, practically all civilizations have engaged in slavery. Black slaves in Africa had black owners. And for well over a thousand years Muslims enslaved untold millions of both Africans and Europeans alike. Jefferson was a man of his time, and we must not discount that fact when recollecting his achievements and scrutinizing his blunders.

Historian Tom Woods, asked the thought-provoking question, "Would you have been an abolitionist in the nineteenth century when abolition parties received two percent of the vote, and lynching's of abolitionists were not unknown?" Likely the individuals who voted to take Jefferson's name off the dinner wouldn't have been, yet they place judgment on a man who has done more for the human race than all of them combined.

35 – ON TORTURE

The American public was recently given information about the CIA's torture of suspected terrorists during the Bush Administration stirring up the debate over whether the torture of detainees was necessary or beneficial to America's security.

The late US Senator Robert Byrd once wrote, "It is our choice as a nation whether to pursue the path of truth ourselves, or leave the details of the abuse to be painfully revealed by others." He went on, "September 11th did not suddenly legalize torture, nor did it exonerate those who authorized such a heinous deviation from the rule of law."

Contrary to the neoconservative views of today, torture was frowned upon by the classical conservatives of yesterday. While facing the wrath of the British Army, George Washington instructed his soldiers to treat the captives with "humanity, and let them have no reason to complain of our copying the brutal example of the British Army in their treatment of our unfortunate brethren who have fallen into their hands." And, during the Civil War

President Abraham Lincoln issued General Order No. 100. This code of military conduct for the Union Army barred torture.

Some politicians and pundits argue that the post 9/11 torture was done out of necessity, but the Revolutionary and Civil War were wars that determined the fate of the United States, yet Washington and Lincoln never found such acts to be of need. If torture wasn't necessary during the most perilous of times in our nation's history, then it's not necessary today.

On April 18, 1988, the United Nations Convention Against Torture was signed by President Ronald Reagan. The ratified convention states, "No exceptional circumstances whatsoever, whether a state of war or a threat of war, internal political instability or any other public emergency, may be invoked as a justification of torture."

Americans must understand that just because one opposes torture does not mean he is apologetic to the Islamic criminals who commit terrorist attacks. We oppose torture because we want a civilized society. We oppose torture because it breeds hate and resentment instead of peace and understanding.

You'll hear supporters of the methods used at Guantanamo Bay claim the techniques worked and now America is safer as a result, although, I don't believe this is true. History has shown that torture has been an ineffective tool in getting intelligence and can have the unintended consequences of weakening a country's national security. For example, the CIA has coined the term 'blowback' which refers to the unintended consequences which stem from our military interventions abroad. In this case, the blowback will be the increased recruitment of Muslims into terrorist organizations and increased terrorist attacks against the west. The acts of torture committed on Guantanamo Bay detainees will be used as a rallying cry to the Islamists.

American veteran Matthew Alexander, who was involved in over 300 interrogations of suspected terrorists, once stated, "I learned in Iraq that the No. 1 reason foreign fighters flocked there to fight were the abuses carried out at Abu Ghraib and Guantanamo." In his interrogations of suspected terrorists, Matthew refused to torture any detainee but was still able to gather significant intelligence. Mathew's position against torture was backed up by a study published in 2014, by Jane Goodman-Delahunty, of Australia's Charles Sturt University when she found that confessions are four times more likely when interrogators implement a respectful stance and build bonds with detainees, versus engaging in torture against them.

For the United States of America to be looked upon as a noble nation by the world's citizens, it cannot succumb to the same authoritarianism, ruthlessness, and cruelty that so many governments have been known for. The torture that took place at Guantanamo Bay is not honorable, nor is it in line with American values. For the United

States to remain the world's beacon of light, we must always hold our government to the highest ethical standards.

36 – ON THE TSA

As citizens, we must not forget the primary role of government; which is to protect our liberties. The sad thing is that many of our citizens do not have this understanding. This statement became apparent when an ABC News poll found that 48% of Americans believed the new intensive pat-down procedure performed by the Transportation Security Administration at our US airports was justified.

Many citizens in favor of legislation that infringes on privacy rights, such as the Patriot Act and the Transportation and Security Act, make the argument that "for our government to keep us safe we must be willing to give up some individual freedoms." That very argument disrespects the American patriots who shed blood, during the Revolutionary War, to fight for the very freedoms that currently so many Americans are so readily willing to abandon.

One must always remember that the greatest security we have is our freedom. Freedom of speech, due process, the right to privacy, to bear arms, to assemble, to make contracts, as well as to own property are the greatest defenses we have against threats. These liberties give Americans a unique identity compared to the rest of the world. The state does not own us, and as a result, we are not at the whims of the state. Our liberties allow us to serve as our own rulers, our own masters, controlling our own destiny.

Last year over 40,000 people died on a US highway and thousands more by natural disasters, but we continue on with our lives with the understanding and acceptance that we may not be here tomorrow.

It's time we dissolve the TSA, give their $6.8 billion budget back to the citizens, and let the airlines provide for their own security.

The most significant security measures our government could implement to protect its citizens from Islamic terrorism is to return to the traditional US foreign policy of non-interventionism, which would decrease hostilities between the United States and Arab worlds. We should also restrict immigration from Middle Eastern countries to the United States and thoroughly vet those who we do allow in to make sure that they are individuals who will add value to our homeland versus detract from it.

37 – ON THE UNEMPLOYMENT RATE

Recently, you may have been staggered to learn that the Indiana unemployment rate supposedly fell to 5.7% in April, according to a tax paid mail-out sent by Republican State Representatives to constituents. GOP cheerleaders were more than happy to circulate this information which, coincidently, was just in time for the upcoming election. However, their deceptive figures won't be able to cast a big enough shadow to hide the many problems of this economy that are in plain view to so many Americans.

A much better indicator of the unemployment outlook is the Labor Force Participation Rate. In 2014, the Bureau of Labor Statistics stated the labor force participation rate stood at a troubling 62.8%. The last time it was that low was 1978. "But," according to Reagan's Budget Director, David Stockman, in the article, "Inside the April Jobs Report," ... "plentiful jobs usually lead to an increase in labor participation especially if it is sustained over time; it's basic common sense."

So why is there a contradictory divergence between the unemployment rate and the labor force participation rate? It is because there has been a mass amount of workers dropped from the US labor force figure, so they are no longer being included in the unemployment rate calculation. In April, 800,000 discouraged workers were dropped from the US labor force calculation. The politically popular U3 unemployment rate, which the Indiana Republicans used in the mail-out, does not include these discouraged workers. A discouraged worker is a person not actively seeking work or who can't find employment within a specified time. Since discouraged workers are not included in calculating the U3 unemployment rate, the cited unemployment rate is deceptively low.

Economist John Williams from ShadowStats.Com uses a traditional governmental method of calculating the unemployment rate, by factoring in discouraged and under-employed workers, a practice which was discontinued by the Bureau of Labor Statistics in 1994. From the calculation, the economist showed the real unemployment rate for 2014 to be around 22%. In his newsletter, Williams wrote, "The unemployment rates have not dropped from peak levels due to a surge in hiring; instead, they generally have dropped because of discouraged workers being eliminated from headline labor-force accounting."

If you're still not convinced that you are being misled by the 5.7% figure, take a look at the employment statistics on Stats.Indiana.edu. In April of 2014, there were only

3,038,501 Hoosiers employed, whereas, in April of 2000 there were 3,070,327 Hoosiers employed, aka there have been more jobs lost than produced throughout a 14-year span. And today, the Hoosier labor force is smaller than it was in 2006, even though our population has increased.

Due to excessive government spending, the private sector is becoming drained of the necessary resources to rebuild our manufacturing base, which is why the trade deficit is widening, and the labor force is decreasing. Just from the fiscal year 2009 to the fiscal year 2013, the Republican-controlled state government increased expenditures from $25.719 billion to $27.766 billion. This excessive government spending is why the jobs being created are mainly tax paid public sector jobs or low paying service sector jobs. This excessive government spending acts as a restraint on the private sector from achieving optimal growth.

Homer Simpson once said, "You can come up with statistics to prove anything, Kent. Forty percent of all people know that." Now I find Homer's statistics amusing, but I can't find Representatives signaling that Indiana has a 5.7% unemployment rate as amusing as I do deceiving.

38 – ON THE UNITED STATES OF AMERICA

The United States of America is a constitutional republic founded on the inalienable rights to life, liberty, and property. The individual is king. America recognizes the right to self-ownership, allowing one to have control over their own body and life. The right to own property guarantees man the fruits of his labor and the title to his land along with the right to liberty which allows a man to live out his own life however he pleases so as long as he is not infringing on another man's rights.

The government was formed by the people to protect their property rights and to provide for a common defense to deter foreign aggression. Peace, trade, and friendship define America's foreign policy and the American commonwealth sides with the Jeffersonian appeals of local rule, sound money, personal responsibility, capitalism, and resistance towards the expansion of state power.

The United States of America as a peaceful nation does not engage in preemptive war, nor perpetual war, only wars of necessity— never choice. America respects the sovereignty of other countries and does not entangle itself in foreign wars. The United States seeks peace for her citizenry by abiding by the foreign policy principle of non-interventionism, and only when an invader threatens America's national security is a declaration of war declared by Congress. Peace is the norm, free markets cover her lands, the state is limited by her constitutional restraints, and government coercion is minimal, which has allowed the citizen to pursue his or her idea of the American dream which, in turn, has enabled the United States of America to become the most prosperous and most free country on this earth.

At this present time in our history though, the United States does not bear a resemblance to this prior Constitutional Republic which was just described. The US military has troops stationed in over 120 nations, and the national security budget has surpassed 1.2 trillion dollars. America is engaged in multiple undeclared wars, using up valuable financial and material resources— resources that could have been used here at home. Wars of choice have sent troops thousands of miles away when instead, they could have been stationed on American soil protecting the borders of our own country from the illegal immigrant flows of Mexico and South America.

How are we to restore the American Republic? The American voter needs to elect principled conservative leaders who will honor their Constitutional oath of office.

To regain our nation's sovereignty, we should reevaluate our defense commitments to foreign countries and end our undeclared wars in Afghanistan and Iraq. Current immigration laws should be enforced and strengthened. The Patriot Act should be repealed. Congress should withdraw all corporate and social welfare funding. And, there needs to be an ideological change among Americans and our political leaders about the role of government.

39 – ON VICTIMLESS CRIMES

The majority of our Indiana citizens have sheepishly accepted the Indiana smoking ban law, never questioning the legislature's true motives.

On July 1, 2012, Indiana, a state ratified on the principles of self-rule, limited government, equality before the law and honoring the private property rights of its citizens, passed a law utterly contrary to these time-honored principles.

Section 23 of the Indiana Constitution reads, "The General Assembly shall not grant to any citizen, or class of citizens, privileges or immunities, which, upon the same terms, shall not equally belong to all citizens." However, instead of the legislature sponsoring equal justice before the law and honoring the states constitution by passing a bill that uniformly applies to everyone, the legislature granted a dispensation. Just like the Roman Catholic Church set aside the law in particular cases for its favored classes, the Indiana legislature has set aside the smoking ban law for its favored classes as well giving exemptions to the horse race industry, fraternal clubs, and casinos.

Such as the excessive tax rates placed on packets of cigarettes, this law is yet another revenue scheme for the state. But just because the smoking law can act as a revenue generating scheme for the government by fining those who abscond doesn't mean the legislature should view it as progress. I feel sorry for the individuals who will be subject to the excessive smoking fines of this new law. The government can measure the revenue this bill will generate, but the government cannot measure the economic and social pain this bill will cause many Hoosiers. This new law has increased the power of the state over the individual. It is an aggress on our liberties.

The Indiana business owner will now be forced to put up nonsmoking signs and remove individuals who refuse to put out their cigarette. If the landowner refuses to comply with these regulations, he or she could face a $1,000 fine. Smoking is a legal activity and should be left to the private business owner to decide whether he or she will allow smoking on their premises.

In a free society, it's the private business owner that has the power to allow or not allow smoking on his land. And, if the smoker doesn't like a private business owner's decision to not allow smoking on his premises, then it's the smoker who has the freedom to take his business elsewhere.

I am not a smoker, but I'm willing to stand up for a man's right to live his own life. This prohibition by the nanny state will undermine respect for the law because it fines behavior many Hoosiers find acceptable and engage in. A country based on individual freedom should recognize a person's free will, not coerce that person into living out another man's will.

40 – ON WAR

In times of war, the private sector laborers' earnings are coercively taken by the state and subsequently distributed throughout the military-industrial complex. This influx of tax dollars allows weapon manufacturers to expand their operations, increasing profits. The influx of tax dollars enable defense contractors to make more significant donations to campaign funds. The tax dollars fund public work-programs for the manufacturing of weapons. The tax dollars allow military contractors to hire lobbyists and financially back the campaigns of war hawks.

Yes, the economics of war brings short-term prosperity to the state and its privileged war beneficiaries. Yet for the masses of Americans, the ones who must obtain their wealth not through coercive taxation but through working forty hours a week in the private sector, this economy of war has led to an economy of peril.

War leads to capital decumulation; when the state takes scarce capital out of the private sector to produce weapons, no longer will the entrepreneur be able to use that capital in his businesses for the benefit of the consumer.

Real capital is scarce. War demands oil, war demands steel, and war demands labor. As the state is employing these resources, economic law forces the prices on them to rise in the private sector. From persistent war, capital becomes scarce in the private sector, leading to higher cost for businesses and higher prices for consumers.

War also leads to currency debasement. The government finances its war deficits by inflating the money supply. As war debts become insurmountable, the government begins to monetize the debt. The Federal Reserve creates the new money for the federal government to pay its war bills, but as the new money begins to circulate, prices adjust upward, and the consumer suffers the ill effects. As the money supply increases, a larger supply of fiat dollars is chasing the goods currently available in the economy, resulting in prices being bid up. The trend of ever-increasing prices in the US economy as a whole is a direct result of the Federal Reserve's inflationary monetary policy.

After World War 1, free-market economist Ludwig von Mises wrote, “War prosperity is like the prosperity that an earthquake or plague brings. The earthquake means good business for construction workers, and cholera improves the business of physicians, pharmacists, and undertakers; but no one has for that reason yet sought to celebrate earthquakes or cholera as stimulators of the productive forces in the general interest.”

41 – ON WELFARE

In his book titled *The Man Versus the State*, 19th century English philosopher Herbert Spencer wrote that the politician "contemplates intently the things his act will achieve, but thinks little of the remoter issues of the movement his act sets up, and still less it is collateral issues." Spencer attributed this problem to the "inadequate intellectual faculty" of the standard politician.

According to a report titled *The American Welfare State* published by the CATO Institute, there are 126 federal anti-poverty programs and approximately one trillion dollars spent annually on anti-poverty programs at the federal, state, and local levels. Now the new trend among leftists is to advocate for even more welfarism by implementing a universal basic income. Former President Obama promoted the idea at the 2018 Nelson Mandela Lecture, and city council members in Chicago have requested that Mayor Rahm Emanuel enact a universal basic income pilot program.

In the late 1960s and early 1970s, Henry Hazlitt wrote two important economic books, *The Conquest of Poverty* and *Man Vs. The Welfare State*, where he made compelling arguments against such government assistance.

One compelling argument Hazlitt made is that welfare erodes the incentive to work, creating idleness, a multitude of unskilled citizens, and decreased economic productivity, "resulting in less real income to be shared by society." Additionally, the high progressive tax rates from the alleged progressive programs would disincentivize our present labor force to give full effort as well. For what would be the incentive to work “long hours” and provide “unusual effort” if any additional income you worked towards would be seized by the State and handed to the indolent?

Furthermore, the trillions of dollars in taxation would place a multitude of burdens on business. For one, the companies that operate at the margins would fail, and the tax burdens would prevent or retard expansions for those businesses that can bear the new rates. The tax burdens would also impact investments in new equipment, thereby voiding potential reductions in cost, reducing the amount of product supplied, or affecting the quality of the product produced. As a result of such impacts, the consumer would be less satisfied, employment would decrease, prices would rise, and US economic productivity would fall. Stefan Molyneux made a similar point in *The Art of the Argument* when he wrote, “Subsidizing helplessness, while taxing productivity, drains society of resources in the long run.”

The trillions of dollars spent on welfare lead to trillions of dollars in government debt; which leads to the Federal Reserve monetizing the debt with the issuance of more currency (inflation); which leads to higher prices; which leads to demands for heightened welfare payments; which leads to more trillions of dollars being spent: a vicious cycle, indeed.

In *Conquest of Poverty*, Hazlitt contends that the angst among the politicians and citizenry to implement such socialistic policies could ultimately destroy the wealth they so yearn to distribute. Hazlitt writes, "The irony is that the very miracles brought about in our age by the capitalist system have given rise to expectations that keep running ahead even of the accelerating progress, and so have led to an incredibly shortsighted impatience that threatens to destroy the very system that has made the expectations possible."

Welfarism also leads to the disintegration of the family. As Molyneux in *The Art of the Argument*, explains, "Single mothers have children largely because the welfare state and other government mechanisms transfer hundreds of billions of dollars to single mothers. (We know this because, as the welfare state has grown, so has the prevalence of single motherhood—and, on the rare times that benefits are curtailed, additional births decline as well.)"

In his online videos, Molyneux explained that due to welfare payments, the State, in many instances, has acted as a financial substitute for the absent father. Due to the availability of welfare, women are no longer penalized if they select a substandard mate, which has led to an increased illegitimacy rate and has damaged children through paternal absence.

Even Franklin D. Roosevelt cautioned that the continued expansion of welfare leads to social disintegration. In his 1935 Annual Message to Congress, FDR said, "The lessons of history, confirmed by the evidence immediately before me, show conclusively that continued dependence upon relief induces a spiritual and moral disintegration fundamentally destructive to the national fiber."

BOOKS MENTIONED IN THIS BOOK

Swords into Plowshares by Ron Paul

33 Questions About American History You're Not Supposed to Ask by Tom Woods

The Church and the Market: A Catholic Defense of the Free Economy (Studies in Ethics and Economics) by Tom Woods

Back on the Road to Serfdom: The Resurgence of Statism by Tom Woods

Nullification: How to Resist Federal Tyranny in the 21st Century by Tom Woods

Free to Choose: A Personal Statement by Milton Friedman

Tyranny of the Status Quo by Milton and Rose Friedman

Lessons for the Young Economist by Robert Murphy

Choice: Cooperation, Enterprise, and Human Action by Robert Murphy

The Conquest of Poverty by Henry Hazlitt

Economics in One Lesson by Henry Hazlitt

Nation, State, and Economy by Ludwig von Mises

Planning for Freedom: And Other Essays and Addresses by Ludwig von Mises

Socialism: An Economic and Sociological Analysis by Ludwig von Mises

Human Action by Ludwig von Mises

The Truth About Muhammad: Founder of the World's Most Intolerant Religion by Robert Spencer

The Politically Incorrect Guide to Islam (And the Crusades) by Robert Spencer

Losing America: Confronting a Reckless and Arrogant Presidency by Robert Byrd

For a New Liberty: The Libertarian Manifesto by Murray Rothbard

The Autobiography of Malcolm X: As Told to Alex Haley

Government by Judiciary: The Transformation of the Fourteenth Amendment by Raoul Berger

The Federalist Papers by Publius (Alexander Hamilton, James Madison, and John Jay)

The Biggest Con: How the Government Is Fleecing You by Irwin Schiff

The Black Book of Communism by Stephane Courtois, Nicolas Werth, Jean-Louis Panne, Andrzej Paczkowski, Karel Bartosek, and Jean-Louis Margolin

The Problem with Socialism by Thomas DiLorenzo

Slavery, Terrorism and Islam by Peter Hammond

Black Rednecks and White Liberals by Thomas Sowell

The Man Versus the State by Herbert Spencer

The Art of the Argument: Western Civilization's Last Stand by Stefan Molyneux

ABOUT THE AUTHOR

Clarence B. Leatherbury graduated from the Indiana University Kelley School of Business in 2012 with a triple major in Management, Human Resource Management, and International Studies. He completed his J.D. degree in 2015 from the Indiana University Robert H. McKinney School of Law. While in law school, he externed for the Indiana Supreme Court and Indiana Attorney General's Office. Clarence is licensed to practice law in Indiana and Kentucky.

Made in the USA
Monee, IL
04 November 2026

67386525R00089